WITHDRAWN

The People of
Penn's Woods West

The People of
PENN'S
WOODS
WEST

LEE GUTKIND

University of Pittsburgh Press

Published by the University of Pittsburgh Press, Pittsburgh, Pa.
Copyright © 1984, Lee Gutkind
All rights reserved
Feffer and Simons, Inc., London
Manufactured in the United States of America

Library of Congress Cataloging in Publication Data

Gutkind, Lee.
  The people of Penn's woods west.

  1. Pennsylvania—Description and travel—1981–I. Title.
F155.G87   1984   974.8   84-2192
ISBN 0-8229-3494-9
ISBN 0-8229-5360-9 (pbk.)

Portions of this book were originally published in *The Georgia Review,*
Pittsburgh Press Sunday Magazine, and *Pitt.*

Thanks also to some of the people who experienced Penn's Woods West
with me; the film crew for *A Place Just Right*—Jan Sedaka, John Rebhun,
Jim Crawford; Larry Peterson for research; Fred Hetzel for guidance; my
friends, Paul Zimmer, Tony Petrosky, Bob Simon, Burt Marks, Randy
McMasters, Larry Caddy, and my brother, Richard Gutkind.

The author
wishes to thank
the Pennsylvania Humanities Council
for its support,
and the
Western Pennsylvania Conservancy
for its guidance and
encouragement.

To Patricia,

For her loyalty and love

Contents

Preface:
Penn's Woods West
Revisited

EDWIN L. PETERSON died in 1972 at age sixty-eight, after a long battle with cancer. But Peterson succeeded in doing what scholars, writers, and historians had been attempting for nearly a century. He put on paper Penn's Woods West.

A professor of English at the University of Pittsburgh and one of the most well-known and respected teachers of creative writing in the country, Peterson received a grant from the Buhl Foundation enabling him to spend a sabbatical year exploring western Pennsylvania, writing of the beauty of its woodlands, the vulnerability of its abundant wildlife, the potential and the travesty of its rivers and streams. *Penn's Woods West*, as it was called when published by the University of Pittsburgh Press in 1958, received complimentary reviews from local as well as national publications, including the *Atlantic Monthly* and the *New York Times Book Review*. It went into a remarkable six printings over the course of eight years.

I never met Ed Peterson, but there are certain things I will always share with him. I teach in Pitt's creative writing program, for instance. I am an avid backpacker, outdoorsman, and wanderer, while Peterson could have easily lived the balance of his life flyfishing, paddling a canoe, exploring the backwoods indefinitely. I have followed in his footsteps before (1977–80) by making a film about western Pennsylvania—*A Place Just Right*—and now, again, by writing a book that in some ways he has already written.

But the commotion of a quarter century of change has made parts of the area about which Peterson wrote unrecognizable, while time has rendered other parts of Penn's Woods West precisely the same.

To Peterson, western Pennsylvania was a marvelous but endangered natural area. He loved the sound of raccoons scurrying at night around his camp, the flash of a whitetail deer streaking through the trees, the sight of a brown speckled trout darting under stones in a clear mountain brook. Repeatedly he warned that we must take steps to preserve them. He linked the future of the city of Pittsburgh to the survival of the mayfly in the upper reaches of the Clarion River. He speculated that timber, although precious, was not nearly as valuable as the humus from which it grows. His words were about wildlife, but his message was to man.

My message is also to man, and *about* man.

To me, western Pennsylvania, this deep bowl of valley framed by New York, Ohio, West Virginia, and Maryland, cut off by the long line of the Appalachians in the east, is a completely separate entity, as different from eastern Pennsylvania as is Kansas from Nebraska. We are not separated by a landmass, however, but by the history, the lifestyle, the attitude and resolve of the people. Whatever it is today and however it has changed over the two and a half centuries since its earliest settlement, western Pennsylvania is a product of the people who have rooted here and carved themselves and their children a home.

When I speak of western Pennsylvania I am not in any way emphasizing Pittsburgh, its largest city. The bone and sinew of Penn's Woods West is in the backwoods—in which we find a mirror of both time-lessness and change. Trappers, mountain men, farmers, and blacksmiths live and prosper in western Pennsylvania, while the steel, aluminum, oil, glass, coal, and automobiles produced here help keep the entire country alive.

There are more whitetail deer in western Pennsylvania per square mile than anywhere else in the world, and there are black bear, mink, fox, muskrat, beaver, grouse, and turkey in abundance. Native Americans live side by side with Lithuanians, Croatians, and Amish. Archeologists and anthropologists have discovered traces of some of the earliest human settlements in North America in western Pennsylvania. In more recent times, the region has been the cradle of the steel industry, the National Football League, and the oil industry. From one end of the country to the other, any of America's many faces—prairie, marshland, sandy beaches, endless canyon, big sky—can be found in western Pennsylvania.

In our own separate travels and in our own personal ways, both Peterson and I came to realize that Penn's Woods West is America writ small.

This book is not only a story of my odyssey in

search of the heart and soul of the people of Penn's Woods West, who are the heart and soul of the land, but also the story of Peterson's *Penn's Woods West*, part of his odyssey renewed and revisited on the twenty-fifth anniversary of its publication.

The People of
Penn's Woods West

Scotty and Mama

AN elderly man with a long white apron wrapped around his waist and a light dusting of flour on his fingertips stepped out of the kitchen and plodded across the room, waving his arms and talking simultaneously. "Mama won't let me sit and talk until I finish baking," he said, nodding in the general direction of a plump, white-haired lady, who was just now gathering checks and counting change at the register.

"Can you imagine?" he asked, smiling mischieviously, pointing and wagging his finger, while rocking back and forth on his heels. "We've been married long enough to raise a family, clear this land, build this restaurant and all the cabins around it with our own hands and our own timber, and still, even when I want to have an innocent conversation with a customer, my wife won't let me."

Scotty was short and wiry with ruddy cheeks and slightly bugged-out eyes that danced as he talked. Ever since I had pulled up on my motorcycle, Scotty had directed toward me an erratic but continuous commentary about the hardships of living with a demanding, domineering woman like Mama. But even when he complained most forcefully, Scotty was nearly always smiling.

I looked up at the old man, returned his smile, and then shrugged sympathetically. I had just devoured some of the best Southern fried chicken I had ever eaten, topping it off with rich apple cobbler. This fellow was an artist with a deep fryer and an oven. My fingertips, which I pondered drowsily, glittered with grease. The wet boots I had placed at the edge of the fire had long ago stopped steaming. My leather jacket, hanging nearby, was now nearly dry. Mama, meanwhile, went about her business quickly and efficiently, finishing her count, stuffing money and receipts into an envelope, without paying the least bit of attention to the protests from her husband.

"Do you hear me, Mama?" Scotty called, his bushy brows scrunched up over his eyes.

The woman, slightly taller than Scotty, cocked her head in an amused but rebellious manner. She had heard her husband, all right—this was a game they obviously often played—but chose not to acknowledge his complaint.

There were about two dozen tables in this lodge, arranged around a great stone fireplace, which divided the room in two. Over toward the front was a row of display cases filled with luscious-looking pies and pastries—Scotty's specialities—and handmade quilts, crafts, and carvings. Over the years, Mama had made it her business to seek out and persuade some of the local folks to preserve and pass on their skills. She, in return, promised to try and sell their wares.

Scotty, who had remained standing by the fire, continued to shake his head and rock back and forth on his heels, watching and mumbling as Mama, the day's receipts in her hand, headed toward a tiny

4

office near the back of the building. "Scotty, we must have tarts for tomorrow. You promised," she said, not unkindly. "You better bake."

"I'm preparing to do just that, Mama," Scotty answered in a singsong, high-pitched whine, followed by a long, drawn-out sigh. "Right after I rest my feet." Clearly, he had mastered the role of the put-upon overworked husband to perfection.

He waited patiently until she closed the door behind her, then walked over to my table, moving in an abrupt and almost mechanical way, as if he were in pain, although his face did not show it. He paused, cocked his ear, and waited a little more, listening while she got herself settled. Then he pulled up a chair and sat down. "You know," he said, in a hushed tone of confidentiality, "I haven't been living up here in the backwoods all my life."

Facing the fire, Scotty sighed, shook off his slippers, and wiggled his old toes at the coals.

Scotty told me about how it was, growing up in Scotland and, as a teenager during World War I, working in the mines for a few dollars a day, ten hours straight, and how, suddenly, he realized he could no longer make himself shimmy into those dark and endless tunnels, no longer face the stifling, claustrophobic danger for one more day. "Not an hour, not even a minute," he emphasized, pounding the table with his fist. "I knew—I don't know how, but I knew—that if I went back in there I'd never come out again."

He gathered up his belongings and went to America, settling in Cleveland, where he eventually found work in the public library. "We were a poor family, with no money or worldly goods, but my mother passed on a treasure of knowledge to me. She taught

5

me how to bake, how to read, how to sing. With those simple gifts, I've been able to earn most everything I ever wanted in my life here in America—and a lot more than I expected." He streched his short, wiry frame across the table, grasped my arm, and squeezed it. "Let me tell you how."

It was past 10 P.M., early spring in western Pennsylvania. I was the only customer remaining in this rustic old lodge and restaurant in the heart of Cook Forest, a tract of 8,200 fertile rich acres fed by the winding Clarion River running through it. Originally called "Rivière au Fiel," meaning "River of Hate," and later, "Big Tobeco," the Indian word for alder, a tree whose bark was used for dying and tanning, the river was renamed in 1817 for its clear distinctive sound, reminiscent of the pure tone of the clarion.

Once a part of the wilderness that stretched from the rocky black surf of Maine to the gentle slopes of the Midwest, Cook Forest was thick with stands of virgin or Weymouth pine, one hundred fifty to two hundred feet high, then the largest and most impressive tract of trees east of the Rocky Mountains. Because of their height, light weight, and resiliency, these white pine were extremely valuable for shipbuilding, especially for masts.

The first settler to take advantage of this motherlode of timber was John Cook, who built a sawmill on the banks of the Clarion in 1826, logged the area with teams of oxen, then rafted or floated his timber down the Clarion to the Allegheny River and into Pittsburgh, some hundred miles southwest. But, within fifty years, the big lumber barons who had followed Cook into the area had already moved out. The forest was still lush and beautiful in parts, rich with hemlock, beech, birch, and maple, but aside from three remaining stands—not more than a few hundred acres in all—the valuable virgin pine was gone.

In 1910, Cook's grandson, Anthony Wayne Cook, attempted to transfer ownership of the family's 6,000 acres to the Commonwealth, which would then be responsible for the preservation of the entire forest, the virgin white pine included. Cook's idea quickly caught on. The Cook Forest Association, a group of naturalists and businessmen, raised $200,000 to improve Cook's property so that the legislature would be more likely to accord it state park status. This was accomplished in 1928, a century after the elder Cook first arrived.

I had never met Scotty and Mama before and, in fact, had no intention of stopping at their lodge. But, after a long and solitary winter, I had opened my eyes one morning and knew it was time to escape. The claustrophobia, frustration, and self-pity that settles in after an awful February in a cold gray city was too much to take. I packed my saddlebags, gassed up my motorcycle, and thundered out of town. I needed to view the world from a different perspective, and to be alone—not just alone in a room of a house or in the corner of a bar, but in a fresh open space. Cook Forest, less than two hours north of Pittsburgh, was perfect for such instant and soothing isolation.

My plan was to camp at a secluded spot I knew along the Clarion, hangout for a few days, and think. But as I paralleled the winding line of the Allegheny River north from Pittsburgh, it had started to rain. I stubbornly continued riding as the rain turned to sleet. Before I knew what was happening, I was lost in the middle of Cook Forest, immersed in the white, blinding blur of snow.

I have hiked the deserts of Texas and New Mexico on hot dry days when the wind suddenly whips up the sand in such a fury that seeing your hand in front of your face is nearly impossible. I have been on a Montana plain and watched at a distance as a tornado inked out the sky. But I have never seen snow and ice come with such sudden ferocity, such compassionless treachery, as it does when it swoops into the mountains of Penn's Woods West.

Luckily, on this particular evening, I sniffed out the warm, soothing smoke of a wood fire. Slipping and sliding, I followed my nose to Scotty's.

First Scotty told me of his comfortable, albeit lonely life in Cleveland, cataloguing and lending books by day and reading those that looked most interesting until late into the night. But when the Great Depression hit, public services were immediately cut back. Eventually, Scotty lost his job.

With no work and a dwindling supply of dollars, he had no choice but to go to the country to look for a livelihood. "I could have stayed in Cleveland, living from soup lines, but a man can't amount to much when he can eat for free. Many of my friends were heading west, but I had often gone camping in Cook Forest during summer vacations, so I decided to go there, deep into the mountains. After all, California was three thousand miles of dust and Depression away, while Cook Forest was less than two hundred. So," said Scotty, "I started walking."

He paused to light a cigarette, staring out the window and into the snow with distant, fire-reflecting eyes. I watched him carefully. I wasn't certain how much of Scotty's story to believe. The more you hang around in the backwoods, the more you realize that there are those who spend idle hours carefully constructing family and personal sagas which grossly exaggerate real life. But it didn't matter to me right at that moment, for I was completely caught up in the romantic notion of it all. This man had obviously told the story of his life many times before; the tale was well timed and well structured. Deep down you could sense, by his force and conviction, that this was more than just a desire to talk or entertain. Scotty may well have been exaggerating here and there, but he obviously felt deeply his every word; he relived with vivid intimacy each scene he remembered and created. "Go on," I said.

"Well, it was tough walking," Scotty continued. "Everywhere you went, people were poor. When I was hungry, I picked berries from bushes, green apples out of trees. Where I could, I chopped wood and performed other odd jobs for my dinner." Sometimes he slept in barns or haylofts, other times concealed himself in the woods, lying down between green sheets of wild rhododendron, on beds of minty fern. "Back then, there were bandits, desperate and forlorn fellows for the most part, but just as dangerous as those in the Old West. Poverty and hunger can make crooks and robbers of us all, one way or another."

It was a long up and down walk across Ohio and into Pennsylvania, heading southeast. He followed approximately the same meandering direction of western Pennsylvania's first toll road, incidentally, the Erie to Waterford Turnpike, constructed in 1809, today a part of Route 19. From there, he took the William Flynn Highway, now Route 8, south through Crawford and Venango Counties and into Titusville. Along the way were tiny pockets of Amish settlers,

9

gaunt and ominous in their black suits and hats; unemployed miners, huddling like hobos around meager fires; shoeless children, begging, sometimes stealing, from farmers who themselves could hardly afford feed for horses necessary to harvest even a bare minimum of food. Here too was the site of Colonel Drake's well, the first commercial oil well in the nation. Brown, rusted derricks, dormant for decades, were everywhere back then, silent sentries guarding a failed and senseless past.

The Cook Forest–Clarion County area had little oil, but was rich in natural gas, the base of a highly profitable industry in the late nineteenth century but, at the time, no longer in great demand. Pipes, rotting and rusted, extended every which way, spidering miles deep into the woods.

"By the time I got to the forest, not too far from where we're sitting, it was pitch-black in the dead of night," Scotty said, dragging from his cigarette.

"You had nowhere to go?" My voice sounded hollow; it had been a long time since I had said anything.

Scotty nodded. "I walked into the woods and laid my bedroll down. It was comfortable enough, although much too damp. I was in a stand of virgin pine. I remember because the pine needles cushioned the forest more than a foot deep." It was quiet and fairly warm. Scotty couldn't see the moon because the tops of the trees were literally wrapped around one another in an umbrella of darkness.

"I was awed by the power and brilliance of those trees," he said. "Their size and their history were both frightening and exhilarating. Even to this day, after having been in the forest now for so long, and always seeing them, I am still awestruck. The feeling never leaves me."

Lying on the forest floor, Scotty closed his eyes and tried to sleep, but he was worn-out from all his traveling and more than a little scared. And now the realization had set in. He was completely on his own. Nothing separated him from absolute poverty except the clothes on his back and the few dollars in his pocket. What friends he had were in another world, hundreds of miles away. Gradually, he drifted into a troubled sleep.

"In the middle of the night, I woke up." Scotty lowered his voice to a whisper and cocked an eyebrow, pausing dramatically in the silent, shadowed room. "I was convinced that I heard the sound of a rich sweet chorus of voices."

"In the woods?" I asked.

"I wasn't sure," Scotty said, pausing briefly once more to tighten the screw of suspense. "So I lay there on my old brown blanket, my eyes tightly closed, my heart thumping, listening until I knew it was true."

"People were singing?"

"It was gospel!" Scotty said.

"But who?"

Scotty slammed his fist down on the table and rolled his eyes in amazement. "Exactly what I wanted to know. Who in their right mind would be singing gospel—or anything else, for that matter— out in the boondocks in the middle of the night?"

Scotty paused to snub out his cigarette. He looked me over carefully to be sure he was commanding my undivided attention. He didn't have to worry. I was hooked.

"I lay there and I listened," Scotty repeated, still whispering, "but the sound didn't go away." The echoing harmony filtered through the forest like a gentle breeze. "I finally opened my eyes and stood

11

up. I could see the faint flicker of a campfire off in the distance, so I gathered up my bedroll and started walking toward it." He paused momentarily to ponder. "Although I had never considered myself a spiritually lost person, I tell you, right at that moment, I quite literally felt saved."

As he told his tale, Scotty had slowly gotten out of his chair and climbed to his feet. He tiptoed, stoop-shouldered, cautiously edging toward the middle of the dining room, just as if he were feeling his way through the forest. I watched him, step by step, and waited, as he went through his lengthy charade. I could picture him hunching behind a tree, parting the leaves and peering out into the darkness.

"It was a midnight gospel service," he announced, his voice filled with wonder. "Even from far away, I could see the congregation, fifty or more, gathered in a circle. I was drawn to them by some mysterious force. I could feel it pulling at me. I began to run," he said, rotating his elbows and knees back and forth slowly, an old man's movement, but with the slightest hint of a steadfast jog. I wondered again, judging by his stiff, awkward motion, if he were in pain. "By the time I made it through the trees, the service was nearly over. But somebody had already caught my eye."

Suddenly, he took two quick steps toward me. Instinctively, I jumped back in surprise.

"A woman." His arm shot up in the air as he raised his voice. "The most glorious and gorgeous woman I had ever laid eyes on in my whole life. I felt the lightning and thunder reverberating from my temples . . ." He paused to look up at the oak-beam ceiling, hesitated, then cast his eyes down to the floor ". . . to my toes."

"What did you do?"

"I couldn't help myself," Scotty shook his head ferociously. "I walked right out into the middle of the circle of those worshipers and stared at her." He paused once again, and a golden glow crept across his face.

For a long while, I sat back, smiled, and waited, savoring the sauce of suspense. As a storyteller, Scotty's timing was impeccable. "And then?" I finally said.

"I started singing," Scotty said. He straightened his shoulders and plodded over to the window.

"Singing?"

"'Ah, Sweet Mystery of Life.'"

"What?"

"It's a love song," Scotty answered curtly, looking me up and down with disbelief. "It's the most romantic love song ever written." He rattled off a few bars.

> Ah, sweet mystery of life at last I've
>   found you.
> Ah, at last I know the secret of
>   it all.
>
> All the longing, seeking, striving
>   waiting, yearning
> The burning hopes, joy and
>   idle tears that fall.

"I'm sorry." I shrugged in embarrassment of my ignorance. "It's nice," I added.

"You better believe it."

When his song was over, Scotty walked slowly across the circle, made yellow by the glow of fire, until he stood right in front of his mysterious lady. I could detect a special glint in Scotty's eye, as if that very night was right now repeating itself in this room, as if that wonderful woman was waiting impatiently for him on the other side of the glass.

"Everyone was watching us now, but it didn't matter a bit," Scotty said. "It wouldn't have mattered if I was in the middle of Carnegie Hall with thousands of people watching, because I felt completely alone with her at that moment, and she was obviously completely comfortable with me. When I finally stopped singing, I reached out and offered her my hand."

"And she took it?"

"Of course." He looked at me suspiciously, but continued. "She took my hand," Scotty said, "and then she got to her feet and stared right into my eyes, and I knew—I knew with more certainty than I had ever known anything in my entire life—that this was the woman I loved and would marry."

"And did you?"

He rolled his eyes and winked at me. I was getting anxious to hear the end of the story, but Scotty would not be hurried. It was his story and he would go along at his own pace, whether I liked it or not.

They spent the rest of the night staring into one another's eyes and talking. At daybreak, they walked up to Seneca Rock, a jutting rocky shelf high above the rippling river, to watch the sunrise. Below them, the Clarion rushed on down toward its eventual union with the Allegheny, blazing with new morning light.

They ate salmon for breakfast, Scotty said. Right from the can. And they got to know each other, talking quietly, like old friends. He learned that she had organized these midnight gospel services all on her own, that her father was a minister, and that she was here with a girlfriend, on vacation from Ohio.

She loved Cook Forest, she told him, and wanted someday to live here.

After the narration of the story of his own life, Scotty demonstrated for the lady the two additional languages he had taught himself over the years while working at the library—French and Russian. He looked at me. Grinning, he planted his hands on his slender hips, tilted his head back, and raised his thick old brush of a brow in the barest hint of pomposity. "I was brilliant," he announced.

They were married within the year, found jobs, and were eventually able to save and borrow enough money to purchase fifty acres near Cook Forest. "Our first buildings were surplus army Quonset huts, purchased in South Carolina and hauled north in an old truck I had managed to salvage and piece together. We hired some of the local folk to put up the huts, paid them by the hour. The first hut took half a day, the second took three days, and the third hut took an entire week to put together. By the time I realized what was going on, we were nearly bankrupt."

Scotty chuckled and shook his head. "I should have known better," he said. Then he laughed right out loud. "After all, these were my own people, just a few generations removed."

Although the eastern part of the state was settled primarily by the English and Germans, the first settlers to take hold in western Pennsylvania were Scotch. Many Irish also made their way over the mountains and into western Pennsylvania—Ulster folk from the north, Presbyterians like the Scotch. The Scotch-Irish were perfectly suited for the wilds of what was then the western frontier, hard drinkers, tough fighters, cagey traders, and prudent busi-

15

nessmen, a legacy Scotty had obviously carried with him over the ocean and eventually into the woods.

Although he had been cooking and baking for himself and for friends through most of his life, he had only started doing it for money when people renting his huts ran out of food or didn't feel much like preparing their own meals. But he was diligent, hardworking, and talented. And so, it didn't take long for Scotty's Restaurant to catch on, not as long as Mama was around, keeping him in line.

"Eventually, we tore down the huts and built these nice cabins behind here, each with its own stone fireplace. Then we put up this lodge, with a fancy, well-equipped kitchen." He stomped his foot, as if to emphasize the solidity of his efforts and investment. Then he paused. "It was a thrill at first; it still is, I guess. But like any other business, it is constantly demanding. Something always comes up."

His voice trailed off right then, as if he suddenly realized that the whole idea of making money doing what you very much liked to do tarnished the fun, if ever so slightly.

Now we both sat, listening to the silence that rang so loudly in the room. For a long time, neither of us moved. The fire had died down to a purring, hissing breath of coals, but Scotty continued to gaze out the window. Out front, at the hitching post, snow blanketed my motorcycle. The round, pale moon made the untouched white of the road look silver. A solitary deer had pressed a ribbon of delicate hoof marks along the side of the building.

A few years later, I learned from a mutual friend that Scotty had been suffering from a long illness. Those bugged-out eyes and painfully difficult movements I had observed were results of a series of small strokes suffered over a period of years, strokes that eventually hampered his ability to move about, to remember past events, or to think clearly. He was not that seriously affected when I met him, although the damage began to take its toll soon after.

Eventually, Scotty and Mama sold their beloved lodge and cabins and went off to Scotland for a long visit. According to Mama, who still lives down the road from their old restaurant, Scotty was aware of what was happening to him and was confused and frustrated by his inability to control it. "As time went on, the strokes continued with increasing frequency. He became frightened of being alone. 'Don't ever leave me, Mama,' he'd sometimes cry out. I never did."

In 1977, Scotty died.

These days, Mama works part-time at the Sawmill Craft Center in Cooksburg, the site of John Cook's original mill, now reconstructed—a project for which she raised money and subsequently helped launch. Extraordinarily healthy and ambitious, Mama is now deeply involved in church-related projects, as well as other religious and cultural activities in the forest. Her newest idea is to raise money to build a gigantic amphitheater for dramatic performances under the stars, and to reestablish regular midnight gospel services. As of now, there is an Easter sunrise service at Ridge Camp, drawing thousands of worshipers, but Mama wants religion in the forest year-round. Perhaps she envisions a time and a place when other men and women, lost and lonely like Scotty, might stumble into the light of love.

A decade has gone by since I first met Scotty, but I

have never forgotten that night, the wonderful story he told me, and our last few moments together in that silent, shadowed room. He was standing at the window, staring out into the silver bed of snow, watching the moonlight bathe the distant hills and trees. He stood there for so long, and concentrated with such force, that you could almost hear the jangled music of his mind as he relived the previous forty years of his life.

Then we heard a scrape against the floor from the next room. The door of the tiny office into which Mama had disappeared some time before opened a wee crack. "Scotty? Where are you? What are you doing?"

Scotty turned ever so slowly away from the window, but he did not answer. Instead, he padded back toward my table, shoved his old feet into his slippers, and paused to look at me. Fireflies darted and danced in those bugged-out old eyes as he stared. Then he turned and headed into the kitchen, pushing his way through the swinging doors.

"Scotty?" Mama called again.

Instantly, pots, pans, dishes, and silverware began to clatter. I heard water running, cabinets opening, the thump of a refrigerator closing, and the groan and squeak of an oven door. It was then that he started singing. I knew what the song was going to be before the first word registered. His rich tenor voice filtered into the room, wrapping me in a cloak of reassuring comfort.

One-Arm Blacksmith

ONE cool white dawn, the blacksmith and his brother went out hunting rabbit. This was the blacksmith's first excursion into the woods since he had left the land on which he, his brother, and their father were born and raised, to take his wife to Pittsburgh to the hospital. All through the months of treatment, and the unsuccessful operation that followed, the blacksmith had fixed in his mind a portrait of this land, soaked in the soft subtle brilliance of autumn.

They stopped at the crest of a hill to look down into the empty, shadowed fields. Far off in the distance, they saw the sun slowly edge its way up the mountainside, pouring light into the slumbering valley. They watched without moving or blinking as the sunlight penetrated the fog, glazing the grassy hills and fields, the clapboard barns and weathered rooftops, the thick stands of sturdy oak and shimmering silver hemlock in a vague scrim of misty gold.

For a long while, the brothers, comforted by the blood of the land that they shared, were lost in thought. They listened as the birds sang songs in solo to the crisp, clear morning. The crickets were a chorus of buzzing ghosts in a sea of weeds and grass. Suddenly, a rabbit broke from the brush and dashed into the open space directly behind the blacksmith. Instinctively, his brother whirled, threw the shotgun up to his shoulder and squeezed off.

An explosion charged through the valley. Thirty-seven tiny lead balls, number four shot, tore off the blacksmith's arm.

Months after the accident the blacksmith was outfitted at a clinic with a double utility hook for a right arm, but the whole contraption wasn't worth an honest day's work. So he got together with his brother one weekend, and they locked themselves up in the shop. In a couple of days they had designed and engineered a new right arm. They made the elbow socket out of airplane landing gears, forged the wearplates out of stainless steel. They also refitted all of the blacksmith's tools to bolt directly onto the hook of his arm with a clamp.

"It all worked perfect," the blacksmith said. "When you come right down to it, no man needs two arms to run a hammer."

"It must have been difficult for you to adjust," I said.

The blacksmith shrugged, then turned to look at the blue ocean of sky above the hills. He seemed puzzled by my question, as if he had never really thought much about having but one arm with which to live.

"Hardest thing to figure out was tying my shoes."

"Really?"

"The only way I ever missed my arm was playin' a

guitar," the blacksmith said. "And I never made a dollar at that in my life."

He reared back his head and burst out laughing. I took a step backward, but he stomped after me until we faced each other, shoulder to shoulder. The blue-black steel blade of his arm rested under my chin.

"Best damn arm in the country." His breath was raw, moldy with snuff and pipe tobacco. "But you know, when you put the human body up against the toughest steel made, there's still no comparison. Steel wears out sooner or later, but the hand lasts a lifetime."

The one-arm blacksmith swung his hammer in short, awkward arcs. The nearly molten metal he was shaping from a raw hunk of cold-rolled steel glowed like a lonely bar of neon, iridescent orange.

His second wife, twenty-three years his junior, stood behind him as usual, wearing large asbestos-covered gloves. She was holding a set of gunmetal-gray tongs, with which she steadied the glowing bar of steel against the anvil.

She was short and round with long gray-streaked hair, pale skin, and eyes of searing blue. You could tell that at one time she had been very pretty, although now her face betrayed a weariness beyond her years.

The one-arm blacksmith explained that he was making a set of chisels for the Amish stonemason who lived down in the next valley. "I tried to tell the man I was busy . . ."

"He's got enough work," the woman interrupted, "he's behind five years."

The one-arm blacksmith had a hunching shuffle of

21

a walk that made it seem, as he kicked his way through the dirt around the anvil, that his suspenders were buttoned to his boots. Wherever he went, the wife dogged his steps. Often she talked for him, or echoed his words.

The place was heaped with tools and machinery, waiting for repair. Parts for a wood splitter he was designing for a farmer down the road were laid out in the corner on a workbench, gathering dust. He was also in the midst of treating a car with a secret ingredient he had recently concocted to retard rusting. "It works," he raised his hook to the heavens. "I swear to God." When the blacksmith invoked the good name of the Lord, he meant it.

"When my people first came to this part of the country, there were no blacksmiths for miles around. But nowdays, there ain't much call for a full-time smitty, so I do what I can to make a dollar. I repair roofs, raise barns, fix bridges. I also done a good bit of shootin' in my day. I was a heavy shooter for the Atlas Explosives Company," he added.

"He blew up half of the hills in this county," the wife said.

Once again, the old man threw back his head and laughed. His cheeks were weathered with wrinkles, creases, and seams. The design drawn by life on his face was one of a kind, as were his eyes, watery and mournful, like those of a human basset hound.

"He's also a crackerjack automobile mechanic, although he don't approve of cars because they knock down sociability."

The blacksmith dropped the bar of molten metal into a pan of water and listened to its sizzle. He took a red checkered bandana out of his pocket and mopped the perspiration from his neck.

"People buy themselves an automobile, first thing you know, they drive past their neighbor," said the blacksmith.

"Radio and TV make it worse," said his wife. "Puts everybody off by themselves."

His mother always had a quilting frame set up in the living room, he said. "The neighbor ladies never had more fun than when they got themselves a quilt goin'. They would come into the front door of our house any time they wanted to sit and talk and quilt. This is how they come to know one another."

The blacksmith said that if it wasn't for his mother's quilting, the Methodists in the area might never have had their own church building. "The ladies sent out letters asking for donations to the building fund in return for having contributors' names and addresses stitched in red silk thread on a special name quilt. There was names from people in every state of the union on that quilt by the time it was all finished."

At the dedication ceremonies, they put the name quilt up for bids and the blacksmith's father insisted on buying it. "The name quilt was my mother's masterpiece ever after. It was kept in the old cedar chest in the living room, but was taken out every Sunday for the people who come to see it. My father swore up and down that that quilt would never leave the family," the blacksmith said.

"Where is it now?" I asked.

The blacksmith turned to his wife, but she shrugged and sighed. "I haven't the slightest idea."

We had dinner in the house, a sagging box of weathered wood, frayed tarpaper, and rusty nails, then went out onto the tiny porch to sit. A rooster crowed from the chicken coop behind the outhouse. "You keep any other livestock?" I asked.

"Last time I raised a beef cow, it dressed out more'n a thousand pounds." The blacksmith looked at his wife, sitting on the edge of the railing, and leaning against the corner of the house. "She fed it for me."

"Never again," she snorted, "not when you consider what I had to go through. We didn't have a place here to keep it, so we took it to that old barn." She pointed across the road at the gray silhouette of a building, partially hidden behind a row of trees. "It was rundown to beat hell. We had to rebuild part of it, just to keep the damn cow dry."

"But that's just a short walk," I said.

"It ain't so short in January when it snows about two feet and you gotta roll the water pan all the way back here just to thaw it out. I won't raise another beef cow," she told him, "unless there's a place to put it on our side of the road. Besides," the woman continued, "it ain't safe crossin' the road no more. After six o'clock, everybody in this county drives like they're drunk."

"They probably are," said the blacksmith. "I wouldn't doubt it."

"Why don't you just buy that place?" I asked. Directly to the left of the barn was an old frame house, sagging in the middle. There was a "For Sale" sign sunk into the ground near the front steps.

"Next place I go," the woman said, "I want to be out of sight of where I've always been."

The blacksmith began searching for a kitchen match. The battered fingers of his one good hand climbed in and out of his shirt pocket before finding one. He struck the match against the dry, unpainted surface of the old porch, puffing as the flame ducked and danced over and under the head of an old briar pipe clamped between his teeth. Smoke tore out of his broad nose, nostrils flaring like wings behind a great, hooking blade of bone.

"Last year," the woman said, "the people that rented that place wrote dirty words all over the walls and ceilings."

"That damn drunkin' bunch of trash," said the blacksmith. "They smoked marijuana."

"The place has a dopey smell to it yet," said the woman.

"You go in there and you can't take a full breath. You gotta come right back out to get your brain straight," said the blacksmith.

The woman turned to her husband. A good deal of the weariness that was part of her face faded at the very thought of her former neighbors, and her eyes were shining. She looked at him questioningly. "Should I say it?"

The blacksmith began puffing his pipe with increased energy. "Why not?"

She looked right at me, blushing all the while. "It smelled like a whorehouse, and I don't even know what a whorehouse smells like."

"It's just the way you imagine it," the blacksmith informed her.

"And how do you know?"

The blacksmith winked. "I ain't sayin'."

The blacksmith waited in silence as his wife walked into the house to start the dishes, then pointed a craggy, battered finger up and over a line of fence toward a grassy plateau, nestled in the slowly setting sun.

"It was nothin' to see fifty kids bobsleddin' in the winter or playin' baseball in the summer over there," he said. "There was once a ball diamond in every town around here and a team to go with it. We had three games a week. Old folks who didn't like baseball met at the schoolhouse for evening debates. People would all read up on a subject in advance, then take sides and argue like hell. It was something to see, them old codgers who could hardly walk, breathin' fire and brimstone at one another for hours on end."

The blacksmith's family had once owned this land as far as you could see. His grandfather had bought it with his mustering-out money from the Union Army after fighting the Confederacy five years. "He paid three hundred dollars for one hundred fifty acres," the blacksmith said. "His name is carved in the bell-tower monument at Gettysburg." Most of the original land is now gone, divided among two generations and subsequently sold off to pay debts.

"After Saturday's baseball game, we went on hay-rides. You'd lay some straw out over the floor of your wagon or sled, meet at somebody's farm, hitch up a team of horses, and start off, ten couples or more. It was all planned out by the girls. They made home-made ice cream and decorated Red Jones's barn for dancin'. It was the biggest and nicest barn for miles. I'll never forget how pretty that barn was.

"We'd head on back about 12:30 A.M. I had to bring the team up to the farm—it was two and a half miles from town—blanket and curry them down, give them a good dry bed, feed them, before I could sleep myself. I'd always have to wake up my dad, go past his bed. 'Dad, I'm in, I'm home.' That's all he ever wanted to know. Whatever I did was my own business, as long as I never embarrassed the family, and got home in time to be rested for church or work in the morning."

The blacksmith whirled around and motioned with his hook at the wagonshed, the outhouse, the main house, his workshop, one by one. "Red Jones's barn is in all my buildings," he said. "After Red died, I heard that his relatives was plannin' to tear down the whole place, barn and all. They was from the city. People with no damn respect for anything old, no matter how good it was. I went over there and watched them rip it down, then salvaged every piece of lumber I could. Paid good money for every bit of it. More than it was worth. Over the years, I built these buildings."

Now the one-arm blacksmith knocked his pipe against the railing. The ashes showered down to the floor. By this time, the sun had slipped behind the mountain. The hill where he had played as a boy, and where he had lost his right arm as a young widower, was black with shadows. For a long time, we sat on the porch without speaking, leaning against the house, waiting for the stars.

"Sometimes I sit here alone in the middle of the afternoon," the blacksmith said. "I look up at that hill and remember my daddy workin' there, stooped over and sweatin'. I close my eyes and listen to the noise of all us kids who played there. I feel the tears comin' up, my eyes nearly burstin'. It's amazing to be so young, and then suddenly to find yourself on the verge of dyin'. You ask yourself again and again, what happened to the years? There ain't never no answer."

The Return of
the Clarion

WHEN Ed Peterson climbed Seneca Rock Overlook and looked down into the green and yellow valley below, he saw the flash of a river, the Clarion, that was once one of the most beautiful in the world. He speculated then on what Red Jacket, chief of the Senecas, might have thought as he stood on this very spot, so close to the broad blue line of the heavens, centuries ago.

"He knew that in its water lived sturgeon, bass and trout, that wild ducks nested among its rushes, that mink, otter and muskrat built homes along its banks, and that the deer and elk found its waters good to drink. But today, the flash we see in the valley is hardly a flash of water. It is the flash of an inky liquid, a contaminated river. . . ."

When *Penn's Woods West* was published in 1958, the river had been nearly destroyed by acid discharges from abandoned coal mines and from sulfurous materials dumped by a paper mill in Elk County. "The Clarion is a pitiable river, close to death," wrote Peterson. People had given up on the

Clarion. Fish could not live in its filthy water. Animals could not drink it. Sportsmen had no interest in canoeing it or camping on its foul-smelling banks. But Peterson continually maintained faith in the underlying goodness of man and his ability to change things, once he recognized his mistakes.

"It will not be long before the Clarion is clean. It will be clean because a growing population and a growing industrial community are desperately in need of its precious purity."

Not long after, the papermill finally launched a concerted drive to reverse its mistakes, while groups of public-spirited citizens spearheaded similar projects on some of its tributaries. Meanwhile, the Pennsylvania Department of Environmental Resources set out to reclaim abandoned strip mines and neutralize acid discharges with lime.

Today, the Clarion is among the cleanest rivers in the state, boasting one of the longest and largest scenic corridors in the eastern part of the country, as rugged, natural, and untouched as it was when Chief Red Jacket looked down upon it.

Not long ago, the directors of the Western Pennsylvania Conservancy, a Pittsburgh-based conservation agency, launched a long-range program to purchase and protect the newly cleansed Clarion River corridor, beginning at Piney Dam, a couple of miles north of the town of Clarion, and extending upriver forty miles, near where the Clarion passes the town of Ridgeway in Elk County.

It is a huge undertaking, a jigsaw puzzle involving many bits and pieces of property. In the southern section alone, from Cooksburg down to Piney Dam, the Conservancy has purchased seventeen tracts of land from individual owners and arranged a compromise with Koppers Company, swapping timber rights on the land in the corridor for rights of equal value on land owned by the Conservancy nearby. Similar to the Cook Forest Association, the Conservancy's objective for all the land it buys is to turn over ownership to a state agency for long-term care and protection.

"Pennsylvania has 45,000 miles of rivers and streams—unmatched by any other state in the lower forty-eight," according to a recent Conservancy bulletin. "But sadly, very few of them remain undisturbed by man's encroachment."

So far, the Conservancy has spent more than $2 million, donated primarily by the Richard King Mellon Foundation, to acquire 4,800 acres along the river, and it hopes to purchase 5,200 additional acres over the next few years. This, coupled with the shoreline owned by state and federal agencies, would protect more than half of the Clarion both from pollution and from major industrial and commerical development.

"As we stand on Seneca Rock this afternoon, sunlight silvers the river, brightens the eastern side of the valley, darkens the western side, and turns the farthest ridge into high light. Far away, a dog is barking; behind us, a chickadee chatters; and high above, an eagle drifts serenely, in possession of the sky. The sounds, the valley, the trees, and the sky are much the same as when Chief Red Jacket stood here. And soon the river, too, will be like this."

River
Road

I have navigated what is perhaps the most rugged and scenic section of the Clarion River, including much of the Conservancy's corridor, without ever once holding a paddle or climbing into a canoe.

Here are miles of silence and privacy, water silver in the sun, tinted green by thick tangles of mountain laurel and rhododendron lining the shore. In the spring, bass and perch are plentiful, darting and diving along the rocky bottom, making puffs of sand rise up through the water like smoke. In the autumn, whitetail deer will tease you. Listen as they spring to life—a wild sound like the straining string of a banjo—and thrash through the underbrush. Watch them idle among the marshes, drink along the banks.

I have made this trip on my motorcycle, but you can do it in a car, once you know the secret of the river road.

The road is not really a secret, it's just that people in Clarion, Forest, Jefferson, and Elk Counties, through which this part of the river flows, keep it pretty much to themselves. And nothing on the state's official transportation map indicates that it exists. There is, however, a mysterious double line running parallel to the Clarion on the map of the Allegheny National Forest issued by the U.S. Department of Agriculture Forest Service. Most of this stretch of the Clarion borders the southernmost tip of the forest.

The road is in two parts. The first is easy to locate and drive. To start, go to the heart of Cook Forest, where you will find a gas station and a general store, a canoe rental outfit, and a number of log cabins. Turn off the blacktop and onto a secondary road, passing the ranger station. Follow the river east into a picnic area with tables and fireplaces. In a while, perhaps no more than a quarter mile, the park peters out, but the road meanders onward.

Some of the most seductive second homes in all of Penn's Woods West are located on the edge of this ragged road bordering the Clarion. Log cabins with magnificent stone chimneys, California-style redwood structures with sprawling sundecks, large A-frames with balconies and screened-in porches. None of the cabins are big or ostentatious, but most are maintained with great dignity, befitting the tall trees and the shimmering river surrounding them.

This road ends abruptly after about nine miles, intersecting with Route 899 where Cherry Run, a popular fishing stream, drains into the Clarion. This is also the point on the map where Clarion, Jefferson, Elk, and Forest Counties—literally half of northwest Pennsylvania—come together.

I once hiked up the hill north, following Cherry Run about half a mile until I came to an abandoned log cabin, built so low you had to stoop to stand inside. Through the trees, I could see an old rusted Airstream trailer in the distance, but I was much more interested in the cabin, empty except for the legs and seat from a broken chair and a couple of pots and pans, old and battered, lying on the earthen floor. I stood in the doorway of this damp, low structure, its walls as strong now as they were centuries ago when first constructed, and tried to picture the rugged and courageous people who came to build these buildings and carve their homes from the wilderness.

Penn's Woods West was America's first post-colonial frontier, the treacherous but promised land to which pioneers struggled over roadless, rocky terrain in Conestoga wagons from the more established eastern seaboard settlements surrounding Baltimore, Boston, New York, and Philadelphia. The great Dan'l Boone pioneered the Kentucky and Tennessee territories only after cutting his teeth under the tutelage of the mountain men of Penn's Woods West. Boone's famous Kentucky long rifle was modeled almost entirely on the Pennsylvania long rifle. Western Pennsylvania set the style for Davy Crockett's lengendary coonskin cap.

Back then, entire families lived many months in half-faced camps, a three-sided lean-to with walls and roof of ash bark in the summer and bear or beaver skin in the winter, until their cabin was constructed. Although they lived in constant fear of Indian attack, the scarcity of supplies was a considerably more serious problem, according to an early settler.

"We wore out all our shoes the first year. We had no way to get more, no money, nothing to sell, and but little to eat, and we were in dreadful distress for the want of necessaries of life. I was obliged to work and travel in the woods barefooted. After a while, our clothes were worn out. Our family increased, and the children were nearly naked. I had a broken slate that I brought from Jersey Shore [a town in central Pennsylvania]. I sold that . . . and bought two fawn skins, of which my wife made a petticoat for Mary; and Mary wore the petticoat until she outgrew it; then Rhoda took it till she outgrew it; then Susan had it till she outgrew it; then it fell to Abigail, and she wore it out."

I was about to retrace my steps down Cherry Run when I first saw Carl Hoskins, who was ninety-one years old.

He came up and out of the rich tangle of laurel behind the old Airstream in which he lived toward the cabin, a faded rucksack flung over his shoulder and a spindly walking stick in his hand. The stick, scraped clean of bark, was bowed out all over like a crippled-up bone, but it held him steady. In fact, it seemed to nearly pull him along.

A retired schoolteacher, Carl was always wandering the woods looking for wildlife. So much of what he remembers as a boy is now gone. Carl's father had seen buffalo grazing in the valleys. He remembered otter, catamount, puma, with their tawny red coats, and the sleek black panther, whose eyes glowed yellow in the night. Carl himself had feasted on the sweet meat of elk, bountiful in western Pennsylvania up through the nineteenth century. He can still hear the sharp, shrill cry of the wolf echo like an eerie dream through the hills.

But primarily because of a state law enacted in 1806 providing a bounty of eight dollars for wolves, panthers, and other predators, most of the animals who once lived here are now gone.

Carl dug his stick into the dirt, dragged himself over to the stream, and let himself down onto the bank in a manner similar to the way firemen slide down their poles. He said that he held no grudges against the hunters who slaughtered the animals or the government that paid them. In fact, he considered the skill and the guile of some of these mountain men truly astounding. Like Jake Guiton, for whom the Forest County town of Guitonville was named.

Jake's reputation as a marksman, then and now an important measure of how mountain men are judged, was unsurpassed. When Jake raised his flintlock to his shoulder, licked his forefinger, and coated his sights with saliva for luck, he never missed. As a teenager, Jake left his cabin one morning with ten bullets his daddy had given him as a birthday present. He returned a few hours later dragging two deer and eight wild turkeys on a sled behind him. Twice in his lifetime Jake killed nine deer with nine bullets, although this impressive feat was quickly surpassed by another settler with the unlikely name of Vogelbacher.

A former gameskeeper in the Black Forest of Germany, and founder of the tiny town of Lucinda, a few miles down the road from Cooksburg, John Vogelbacher is still honored annually in *Ripley's Believe It Or Not* for killing nine whitetail deer with one bullet—the same bullet. Vogelbacher dug the bullet out of each deer as he downed them and used it again.

But one of the greatest of all western Pennsylvania hunters, according to Carl, was Billy Long, nicknamed Long Knife by the Indians. Hunting, and the

35

animals he stalked, was damn near all Long Knife ever thought about. In fact, Long Knife was so good, the animals actually stalked him.

Many an evening, Long Knife would position himself on top of a ridge with a cache of ammunition and a plentiful supply of whiskey to keep him company. About sunrise, he'd spit out his chaw, clear his throat, and begin barking. He had studied the hungry yip and howl of the wolf for so long, not even the wolves themselves could tell the difference, at least not until they would come bounding up the hill toward him. "By that time," said Carl, "it was too damn late."

Except for bear, the panther was the strongest and fastest animal in the forest. Long Knife would often kill a deer, crawl under its carcass, and wait. When a panther came to take the deer for its evening meal, Long Knife would jump up, let out a blood-curdling war cry—and shoot it.

Carl explained that the Indians had always shared generously their knowledge about hunting and planting, at first out of simple kindness and later because of an insatiable thirst for whiskey.

"Bill Long's father, Louis, was the first person to manufacture large quantities of whiskey within fifty miles in any one direction. Louis gave the Indians all they ever wanted to drink. Whenever they sobered up, they'd pay in pelts, tell him things he wanted to know about the woods, or do odd jobs as tokens of appreciation."

Carl paused to let out a long, loud sigh. Now that he had rested a bit, color had returned to his cheeks. His face was clean shaven. His slender veined hands were splotched brown with age. "This country coulda done without the products provided by Louis Long."

Cornplanter, chief of the Senecas, was well aware of how whiskey poisoned his people.

"The Great Spirit first made the world and next the flying animals," Cornplanter once said. "Then he made different kinds of trees, and weeds of all sorts, and people of every kind. He made the spring and the other seasons, and the weather suitable for planting. But stills to make whiskey to be given to the Indians he did not make. The Great Spirit wishes me to inform the people that they should quit drinking intoxicating drink, as being the cause of death and disease."

To get to the second part of the secret river road from Cherry Run, follow Route 899 into Clarington, then turn left on the dirt road—Belltown—that begins across from the Country Store.

The river narrows somewhat as you move further upstream. You pass sandy coves buzzing with dragonflies and grasshoppers, and brown rocks, flat and large like tabletops. The water seems to get thicker and richer as it simmers in the sun, a pure solid reflection of Pennsylvania green, spiced with flashes of yellow dandelions and pastel dots of trillium.

The going gets rough for a while in the area across from Clear Creek State Park in Jefferson County. But workmen are regrading the road right now. By the end of the summer, this stretch will be easily passable. I move on. A rusted pipeline from an old gas well seems to be moving with me, clinging to the edges of the road as far as I can see in either direction. Such pipe is a constant and unavoidable scar through all of Penn's Woods West.

Old towns, ghosts of another era when loggers

37

floated timber downriver to the Allegheny and eventually into Pittsburgh, rise up along the bank. At Milltown, I memorize the mailboxes. Hazel A. Thatcher. Gary Blair. DeWitt Metts. All the while, old men sit on their stoops, watching with somber eyes as I ride by, while children dash back and forth across the road, waving. How nice to be a child with the woods as a playground and the river as your front yard.

Later, a house emerges out of nowhere. It has a freshly painted green porch and sparkling white pillars. An icy spring bubbles down into a lily pond behind the house. I stop, dismount, and drink. In a field near Elliott Run, there's a horse so old it looks like a statue. It pays no attention as I pass. Crossing a cast-iron bridge, black with age, I drive up a road so steep and rutted it's like climbing a washboard wall. I come back down the road slowly, heart pounding. The solitude, the freedom, make me feel breathless. I am not just alive, I am tingling.

Further on, a handmade suspension bridge hangs over the river, leading to another old but well-kept house, also pillared white. Here, the green river loops around in a lazy gracious hook. I lie on the flat brown rocks that extend out over the river and watch overhead while the bridge sways to the silent breeze. I can hear the water lapping the shore, almost feel the fish darting and diving underneath me.

I see the sun slipping down behind the hills. The shadows telegraph the upcoming evening. But it is difficult to disconnect myself from this silent spot and move ahead. I want to drowse indefinitely; I don't want to be put on a timetable, held to a schedule. For the river is magic. Its stalwart music and steadfast

rhythm are riveting and unrelenting. All one ever
needs to see or to learn is in this river, and in all
rivers. The water carries the world on its shoulders—
the riffles of life, the rapids of danger, the pure
shimmering silk of contentment.

Cooper

He came back in one piece, never wounded, but all the same inflicted, the cooper said. The government calls it "agent orange," but to me it's "invisible orange," because I can't see what my son has seen, can't feel what he's felt, can't understand when he blanks out. He just goes away, sometimes for hours, sometimes for days. What scares me is that he won't ever come back. He'll just stare off into the distance forever.

IN the gray faded snapshot, taped to the workshop wall, the cooper is up to his ankles in wood shavings, straddling a tired old contraption resembling a headless hobby horse. This is his *schnitzelbank*, the same schnitzelbank that his great grandfather made nearly two hundred years ago after coming from England to America to practice the family craft of coopering.

"'Schnitzel' means 'whittle,'" the cooper told me, "while 'bank' is 'horse' or 'bench.' The 'schnitzelbank' or 'shaving horse' has been used by coopers worldwide for centuries, but it's the Dutchman's invention."

In this part of Pennsylvania, the Germans and Dutch are often referred to interchangeably.

The cooper's hands are straight out in front of him, and he is holding a drawing knife, its flanged convex blade resting lightly on a rough-cut walnut barrel stave. When he rocks back and forth—a quick but seemingly awkward motion—feathers of wood float to the floor.

In the snapshot, the cooper, much younger then, his slender smooth face shadowed by an old Panama hat, is surrounded by the many products of his labors—butter churns, piggins (for storing butter) buckets, gathering barrels (for sugar water during maple season), in all the different stages of development. The tools of his trade hang in a line from hooks on the wall, like soldiers at attention.

"You start with green wood—hickory, walnut, or oak—and split it with your frow [axe]. You soak it in water for two weeks, perhaps more, until she's so supple, she'll bend. These days, modern coopers use steamers for bending wood, but the real oldtimers just threw 'er in water and kept their eyes peeled. They had the instinct and patience for perfection. No matter how much money you got, you can't buy the right touch. You got to learn it."

After shaping the stave inside and out on the schnitzelbank, temporary bands are inserted around the barrel to hold the staves together while the chime is being set. He held up a large and unwieldy-looking tool, also made by his grandfather, similar to a draftman's compass. The groove into which you fit the staves in the bottom of the barrel is called a chime, which was once called a geik, which was made by this tool, known as a geikriser, the cooper said. You fit the staves into the chime, slip off the temporary metal

41

bands, and pound down your oak hoops with a cooper's mallet. The circumference of each hoop is measured by a tool called a traveler.

"There were no nails or glue in the barrels back then," the cooper said. "A cooper's stove, placed inside the newly made barrel, would shrink and seal the staves together. A bung-borer reamed out your bung or faucet. Straw is burned to char the inside of a barrel if it's for whiskey."

He is one of the few coopers in the United States who works entirely in the old way, completely by hand. "Some people claim I'm the best cooper in the country." He shrugs, smiles slyly, and winks. "I don't know all the coopers in the country . . .

"A young fella came to see me not too long ago. Called himself an artist. He asked whether I used a power saw to cut off the ragged ends of staves before fitting them into the chime. 'Sure I do,' I told him. 'But the power I use for my saw comes entirely from my right hand.'"

The cooper said that young people today think they can apprentice under a master craftsman for a few months and learn all there is to know. "They come to me all the time, beg me to teach them. Then, after a couple of weeks, they try to tell me my business. This artist fella, for instance. He says to me, 'But you can't cut the bottom perfectly straight by using a handsaw.'"

The cooper shook his head, wagging his finger, and spat on the ground. The whites of his eyes were simmering red, as if he was worked up to a fit. "'Well, what the hell do you think I been doing for the last fifty years?' I asked him."

The cooper's voice was sharp and high like a screeching bandsaw. "The kid looked at me as if I had finally made some sense to him. He leaned so far forward in his chair, I thought he was going to fall over. His eyeballs were about as big as wagon wheels. 'I don't know,' he says. 'What?'"

Now the fire in the cooper's eyes faded, as he shook his head back and forth, wheezing and cackling like an old hen. "'What?'" he repeated a couple of times. "'What?'

"Well, I'll be goddamned. Will we ever be spared of the embarrassing ignorance of young people?"

Then, as if the possibility of such salvation suddenly occurred to him, he added, "I hope not."

The cooper took the snapshot off the wall and cupped it in his hand. You could see almost the entire workshop in the picture, taken nearly thirty years ago by a relative, long dead. The gray silhouette of his old truck, sitting in the dust behind the smokehouse, loomed in the window. A little boy in boots, bib overalls, and a baseball cap, stood in the doorway. He was smiling and waving at the camera.

The cooper walked up the steps of his old log cabin and dropped into a squeaky rattan rocker. This was the same log cabin that his great-grandfather had built two centuries ago. During the Great Depression, when his father had to sell off part of their land to pay bills, the whole clan had turned out to dismantle the cabin, move it and rebuild it, log by log, on another corner of the property.

From where he sat, he could see through the screen door and inside the house. The sun streaming through the windows made the front room shimmer. The spinning wheel he had modified for his mother out of a nineteenth-century foot-powered dentist's drill languished in the corner, untouched since the day she died.

Before she got sick, the cooper said, his mother grew her own straw, beat the chaff out of the fiber with the family's old scutching wheel, combed the flax with hackles, and spun and wove her own linen. "On special occasions, when we used the linen for Sunday dinner, I always felt like royalty," the cooper said. His mother also chopped the wood and made all the family clothes.

Just then, a car bouncing up the dirt road jerked him to his feet in one bounding movement. He did not like visitors one bit.

A blonde woman with short hair and hooped earrings got out of the car, smiling and waving. "Howdy," she called. She was wearing a bright colored silk shirt of western design, suede cowboy boots, and Levi pants that choked her buttocks. The cooper stood at the rail and watched as she made her way to the house. "I've been meaning to come and visit for a long time," the woman said.

The cooper stood in silence as he watched her walk the steps. He had never seen her before in his life.

"I've heard a great deal about the work you do," the woman said. "It's incredible."

"Where you from?" the cooper asked.

"Pittsburgh."

"You heard about me in Pittsburgh?"

She laughed and raised up the palm of her hand. Her nails glittered with red polish. "No," she said. "We have a place a few miles from here on the river.

My husband uses it for hunting and fishing. I come up with him sometimes."

The cooper did not hate city people, not their fancy clothes or their shiny cars. He did not hate them for all the money they brought into the area to purchase the property poor folks couldn't afford to keep up. He did not hate them, even though the influx of flatlanders gave unnecessary and frivolous ideas to the young people; even though their presence and their hunger to duplicate the trappings of city and suburban life—paved roads, fancy schools, social programs, complicated septic systems—resulted in taxes which the home folk simply could not afford to pay. Even though it was the city people who started the war, and the poor people who fought the war, he did not hate them.

But he didn't want their money. And he didn't want anything to do with them. It was their own goddamn business what they did with their money, but he didn't have to take it. This he had decided a long time ago. He didn't have to take any money or make things for the people who sent his son to that godforsaken land of swamp and rice.

"It's nice of you to visit," the cooper said. He tried to make his voice simultaneously sad and sincere, but he simply couldn't force himself to smile. "And I appreciate all the compliments, but I don't have anything to sell."

"I wouldn't be too choosy," the woman said. "I mean, it's for a gift. They—the people it's for—wouldn't actually use it."

"They wouldn't use a churn, a barrel, a mug?"

"Well maybe for decoration."

"I see."

45

"I saw that wonderful berry bucket you made for Mrs. Janowski down the road," the woman said. "I would take a berry bucket if you happen to have one left. Mrs. Janowski bought hers just last week."

"Mrs. Janowski is going to gather berries with it," the cooper said.

"She makes wonderful preserves," the woman replied. "I always buy from Mrs. Janowski when I'm up here. I take them to all my friends."

"I'm all out of berry buckets," the cooper said.

"I would buy a churn, I guess."

"I'm all out of churns."

"Do you need any toys?" the woman asked.

"Toys?"

"My husband can get you toys or children's clothes at discount prices . . ."

The cooper stared at the woman. He had nothing more to say.

"Don't you have anything to sell at all?" she finally asked.

The cooper shrugged and sighed as he stared at the blonde lady with the polished fingers and the gold-hooped earrings who had come up onto his porch without being invited to offer him toys.

"I got too many back orders that's keeping me busy," he finally said.

"I can wait," the woman persisted.

"It's going to be a long time."

"I've got time. After all, you do such fine work."

"You ever seen my work?"

"I saw your berry buckets."

The cooper was silent for a long time, watching the blonde lady, who was staring at him, smiling pleasantly. Her blouse was unwrinkled, her boots were

46

new, her lips were perfect. Even her teeth were white and straight.

"It's going to be a very long time," the cooper repeated.

"Just tell me when to come back," the woman insisted.

"Twenty years," the cooper replied.

The cooper's eyes followed the lady's dust down the winding maze of dirt roads to the highway. Then he turned to look at the man—his son—who had, all the while, been sitting in the corner on the front porch floor, in the shadows. He was in his early thirties, pale and gaunt under a three- or four-day bristle of beard. Outwardly, there was nothing wrong with him, nothing you could see, except that the eyes staring off into the deep sun-soaked valley were empty, and the nails of the fingers drumming steadily on the bare wooden floor were bitten down to the bone.

Progress In
Penn's Woods West

IN the back of my mind I knew, even when I first met Scotty, Mama, the blacksmith, and the cooper a decade ago, that part of northwest Pennsylvania was becoming increasingly and uncomfortably commerical. Each time I returned, I noticed the upward spiral of land prices, along with the continued increase of traffic brought about by the completion of Interstate 80, which extends 313 miles through northern Pennsylvania in a straight line from New Jersey to Ohio. Of the 28 miles in Clarion County through which I-80 travels, there are six interchanges—the most of any of the fifteen Pennsylvania counties touched by the road.

During Peterson's time, northwest Pennsylvania was relatively isolated, simply because no major highway linked it to more populous areas of the state. To get to Clarion, Jefferson, Elk, or Clearfield Counties back then, you had to travel up Route 8 through Butler or follow Route 28, meandering along the river through Kittaning and eventually through Brady's Bend. And although the Pennsylvania Turnpike stimulated an economic boom for parts of the Ligonier–Laurel Highlands area, it also brought an intrusion of people—people whose very presence upset the rhythm and balance of a way of life that had remained undisturbed through the previous century. Will history be repeated in Pennsylvania's great northwest?

A partial and discouraging answer came in a single sentence I recently read in a letter from a Clarion County official: "Please note that Clarion County is now referred to as 'Clarion River Country' *for promotional purposes*." The italics are mine, but the reality and impact of these words could well be devastating.

Along with the ever-increasing influx of hunters, hikers, campers, canoeists, and tourists attending the week-long Clarion River Country Autumn Leaf Festival (chock-full of questionable wilderness events, such as a golf tournament and a go-cart Grand Prix), Cook Forest now has twenty miles of trail specifically set aside for snowmobilers, barbarians of the backwoods euphemistically called "outdoor winter adventurers" by the Clarion County Tourist Promotion Agency. Put all that together with the cross-country ski trails, the ice skating pond, the tobogganing hills, the concession shops, "and a wide-open kid-proof wilderness [I continue to quote from agency literature] and you've got the ingredients for more fun and commotion than you've had for a long time."

Fun and commotion, most notably from the snowmobiler, is certainly what the deer and bear, the raccoons and rattlers, and all the other animals, birds, and insects can do without. How long will "the spectacular glory of mountain laurel and rhododendron in riotous bloom" last? How often will we see the

49

"shimmering crystal chandeliers on bushes and trees after freezing rain" with a horde of snowmobilers roaring and thrashing about?

Although this frenzied promotional pitch may well benefit the area's economy in the short run—county officials estimate that tourists spending $34 million annually have generated about eleven hundred jobs for local residents—the overall impact could well be devastating. It has happened in other parts of the United States, places with considerably more resources and wider and more open spaces. Parts of Yellowstone Park in Wyoming and Montana and Mount Rushmore in the Black Hills of South Dakota are as honky-tonk as Atlantic City's boardwalk. Yosemite in the summer is like traveling a Los Angeles freeway on the Fourth of July.

So far, most of western Pennsylvania has been lucky to avoid these plastic palaces and tinsel towns that come part and parcel with too many tourists misled by too much promotion, but if zealous advertising executives and real estate entrepreneurs are not careful, Cook Forest could be the first casualty of the progress in Penn's Woods West.

Cash Crop

WE pulled over onto the shoulder of the road and killed the lights.

"Let's go." Jerry jumped out of the truck.

"Where are you taking me?"

"Far enough to bring the whiskey, but not so far as to open up a new bottle."

We ducked under a fence and climbed up and into an old mud-splattered tractor. Cranking on his machine, we took off over an empty field.

Jerry navigated through the dark by memory. The cool wind felt good against my warm face, but after a while I started to get a little nervous.

"Where the hell are we going?" I asked again. Jerry was being far too secretive, and we were becoming much too isolated for my taste.

"You asked about my crops."

"What about them?"

"I'm a one-crop farmer," he answered mysteriously.

"So?"

"So take a look," he said, just then stopping his tractor and reaching up to switch on an overhead spotlight. The heavy yellow beam cut like a saber through the inky darkness.

At first I didn't quite understand. All I could see was some kind of vegetation, tall and dark green under the heavy glare of the spot. It was a wild-looking crop, uncultivated, planted and grown haphazardly, more like weeds than food. Maybe we were in the wrong place. Or maybe Jerry was putting me on. I didn't quite understand.

Jerry doused the spot, bent down, broke off a stock of the stuff, and handed it to me. "Take a whiff," he said.

I put it up to my nose. The weed had a hauntingly familiar tangy aroma. A great big grin burst across my face. "Well goddamn you," I said. "You sneaky bastard."

"Goddamn right," Jerry answered. He was beaming, confident even now of a comfortable future.

In a few short weeks, if everything went well, Jerry, thirty-six years old, Vietnam veteran, would harvest an entire acre of marijuana.

The Tall Trees

THE Allegheny National Forest, thirty-seven miles long by forty-three miles wide, bordered on the north by New York state and on the west by the Allegheny River down to Tionesta, has always been one of the best-kept secrets in the United States.

In addition to excellent bass and trout fishing, good bear and small-game hunting, and one of the largest deer herds in America, hundreds of miles of hiking trails wend their way through rocks and trees. Backpackers can begin at the New York–Pennsylvania state line, tour ninety-five miles of the forest on the North Country Trail, and hook up to the Baker Trail, which extends southwest more than a hundred miles to the Rachel Carson Trail, within the Pittsburgh city limits. Literally, a Pittsburgher could start in New York and walk all the way home through the woods.

You might also float home down the Allegheny from Kinsua Dam to the Golden Triangle and beyond, as did Peterson twenty-five years ago. Or, you could tour the forest in an automobile, stopping now and again through your journey to experience the beauty, the memory, the mystery of such sacred spots as the oasis of virgin timber and bubbling brook known as Heart's Content.

"As we entered the forest," writes Peterson, "the bright light of the day began to fade into woodsy dimness. A hundred and fifty feet overhead, the crowns of the tremendous trees blacked out the sky, and all around us, as we went deeper into the woods, was that strange stillness of the forest, like the stillness of a fog at night, so quiet that the chittering of a red squirrel seemed raucous and irreverent." (His companion that day was photographer Tom Jarrett.)

"The ground was soft underfoot. Our heels made no sound. Some of the trees, we are told, were tall before the Mayflower set sail from England. To stand beneath them in perfect silence, to be willingly dwarfed, to sense rather than to see their grandeur is a chastening experience. Among these ancient inhabitants of the earth, our mortal pretentions are so out of place that we forget them. They dissolve into the silence and the twilight, and we stand alone and honest and humble among those that take their sustenance from earth and sky.

"For an hour or two, saying very little, we walked among the great ones. Not until we were back at the car, I think, did we speak naturally. Then Tom said, 'It isn't far from here to Ludlow.' He looked at his watch.

"'Let's try it,' I said. He did not know that I had a special reason for wanting to see the Tionesta Forest.

"About ten miles of dirt road brought us to Sheffield; about five miles on Route 6 took us to Ludlow; and then we began the stony road into the largest tract of virgin timber in Penn's Woods West—a mixed stand of hemlock and hardwoods.

Twenty minutes after leaving Ludlow, we again stood among the giants.

"Not far from where we parked the car an obscure trail led down the hillside into the darkness of the forest. We followed the trail for a few hundred yards until it separated into two trails.

"'You try one and I'll try one?' Tom suggested.

"'Let's take an hour,' I said, 'and meet here.'

"Being alone made a difference. It made the trees taller, the forest larger, the silence deeper. Here were not a hundred acres as Heart's Content but thousands of acres shaded by the same trees that had lived here before the frontier fort was erected at the forks of the Ohio, trees that were old before a white man ever saw them, trees that will be here long after all men now living are dead. No wind moved among their distant branches, and no birds sang. If deer, turkey, or squirrels were in the woods, they made no sound."

Peterson stops to sit on a log and rest, and to think back forty years to the time when his father first introduced him to these trees. Initially, he was disappointed—they were just trees, large but ordinary—but as he walked with his father deeper into the woods, he began to understand.

"Although my father was ordinarily a fast walker, we went down the trail slowly. Sometimes he would stop beneath one of the big trees and with his eyes, follow its trunk up to the branches at the top and the bit of blue sky beyond. I did, too. They *were* big trees. I talked a good deal while we walked, but my father hardly talked at all. Once he put the palm of his hand gently on a tree and kept it there a long time. He was just looking at his hand on the tree trunk.

55

"It was dark and shadowy and quiet in the woods, and the spell of it all began to seep into me. In spots, sunlight found its way through the branches and made bright brown splotches on the fallen needles. From down in the valley, a sound came up, a sound like thunder.

"'What's that?' I said.

"My father looked down at me. 'It's a grouse,' he said, 'a grouse drumming.' Then he walked on, slowly, among the trees.

"I had never heard a grouse drumming before, and I wanted to ask him about it, but this was not the right time. To me it sounded more like buffaloes. I had never heard a buffalo, either, but I had read about them and about how, when the herd was moving, it made a sound like thunder.

"Maybe my father was wrong. Maybe a few buffaloes had escaped the white man's notice and the Indian's and were still living there.

"Ahead of me, my father did not look so tall as usual. I saw him stoop down, looking at something on the ground. When I came up to him, he was selecting little hemlock cones and putting them in his white handkerchief.

"'What do you want them for?' I said.

"'I just want them,' he said. 'Maybe I'll plant them in the back yard. I just—want them.' He put the handkerchief carefully into his coat pocket. 'Remind me to take them out of my pocket when we get to the car,' he said. 'I don't want to crush them.'

"As we went on, I kept thinking about the buffaloes and the elk and about the Indians, too. I asked my father about the Indians.

"'It isn't very likely,' he said. 'They're gone now, along with a lot of other things. I wish I could have seen them then, the trees. You couldn't get your arms around them, no, not two of you. They're gone now,' he said, 'except for just a few like these.'

"I was still thinking about the elk and the buffalo.

"'Here,' he said, 'try to put your arms around this one.'

"I tried, just to please him, but I knew I couldn't do it. My arms seemed shorter than usual, and the bark hurt my face. He was pleased, though, that I had tried, for when I turned around he was smiling—a strange smile that seemed to come in some mysterious way partly from him and partly from someone else.

"'But it's a nice idea,' I heard him say, still smiling, 'about maybe the Indians still being here.'

"Where the trail turned uphill, the forest was not so dark. He talked a lot as we were going uphill, but I was thinking of too many things to hear all that he said. When we got back to the road, I turned around to look at the trees again.

"Now that I knew them, they looked different. They were the biggest, the greatest trees I had ever seen. I could still feel the bark under my fingers and the hurt of the bark on my face, and I could see the branches, black and high in the sky. I hoped that they would live forever, that my father would live forever, that nothing would ever die, not trees, nor Indians nor buffalo. I was exalted and sad at the same time.

"My father reached into his coat pocket and said, "'Here boy, have an apple.' He had another one in his pocket for himself. Together, we rubbed them on our pants to make them shiny, and then we ate them on the way back to the car.

"Now, forty years later, I stood in the same forest,

remembering an important boyhood experience compounded of tall trees and quietness and the drumming of a grouse. Little had changed except for the absence of the tall man. Even the exaltation and the sadness were the same, though older and a little wearier."

More than one-third of the people in the continental United States live within a day's drive of the Allegheny National Forest. And yet, hundreds of thousands of easterners crowd the highways, expend millions of dollars in fuel and tolls, suffer through eternally boring and increasingly dangerous interstates on their way west to the Rocky Mountains and beyond to duplicate many of the sites and experiences available to them right here in the Allegheny National Forest in Penn's Woods West.

First Monday

LIKE the Mardi Gras in New Orleans or the running of the bulls in Pamplona, buck season is an institution and a religion in western Pennsylvania. On the first Monday of the thirteen-day season (usually the first Monday in December), factories are in limbo, high schools are devoid of males, mill towns become ghost towns. A million men and some women—more hunters than there are deer—will take to the woods in Woolrich plaid and blaze orange with high-powered rifles, in search of the elusive whitetail buck. For the dedicated hunter, the ritual actually starts much earlier, with a month-long archery season in October, and continues with antlerless season in mid-December, when nearly 75,000 deer are harvested in just two days. There is also a flintlock season for the aficionado, who has undoubtedly been tracking deer droppings and searching out "buck rubs," made when the male deer rubs the velvet off its antlers against the bark of trees, since late last summer. But the high point is the first Monday. Except for Christmas, Easter, and Super Bowl Sunday, it is the biggest blue-collar day of the year.

Larry Caddy's life has always centered on deer hunting. At home in Munhall, not far from where U.S. Steel's Edgar Thompson Works stands in sad and empty silence along the banks of the thick brown mass of the Monongahela River, Larry displays a large collection of guns to kill deer and expensive scopes to help see them better before squeezing off. Larry doesn't trust manufactured bullets. He loads his own and tests them at the gun club down the road. Larry also skins, butchers, and eats the deer he shoots, cures and tans the hide. A fountain of enthusiasm, Larry is probably the only hairdresser in the country who whispers sweet nothings about deer hunting into his customers' ears. Slender, boyish, and handsome, Larry, thirty-eight, has long been happily married, but the one and only woman in his life on first Monday lives in McKean County, four hours north of home.

Widowed some time ago, with two young children, Jenny opens up her small house each deer season to Larry, me, and a few others from western Pennsylvania, and the Browns, a black family from Wilkes-Barre in the east. This includes J. T. Brown, his sons, Calvin and Jack, three grandsons, and Uncle Shorty Mingus, all of whom have worked in the same factory. Although deer hunting is good through most of the state, it is excellent in northwest Pennsylvania, especially in Warren, McKean, and Potter Counties, adjacent to the New York border.

It's a tight squeeze, with two hunters to a bed and four to a room, bodies sprawled every which way in the hallways and across the living room floor. Jenny's children burrow into sleeping bags for the duration of deer season. The twenty-five dollars a day—including breakfast, dinner, and a brown-bag lunch—is essential to Jenny, for she is no longer able to work a full-time job.

The weight and responsibility of raising two children, alone, in the woods, has taken its toll. Jenny is forty-eight, but her skin is tired and gray. Some of her hair is falling out; her arms, cheeks, jowls, and thighs are quivers of fat. Years ago, she lost an index finger on the Wild Slide Ride at the county fair, and with the ninety-six hundred dollars from the insurance settlement bought this house and the few acres around it. Trading in a finger for a lump of cash might have been the best thing to ever happen, for Jenny could never have saved up a down payment in any other way.

To the backwoods people of western Pennsylvania, where unemployment is as high as 30 percent, welfare is a great urban shame, but deer season is an invaluable opportunity to earn extra money. Many families in northwestern Pennsylvania will put up people the first few days of the season—sometimes the same hunters for decades. Motel rooms are booked years in advance. Larry has been staying with Jenny nearly a decade. I have tagged along the past few seasons, while the Browns have been coming ever since Jenny bought the house.

People also haul trailers from the city, camp in the woods in tents, or sleep in their cars on the side of the road. Churches and volunteer firefighters' associations sponsor all-you-can-eat pancake breakfasts for hunters going into the woods first morning, and all-you-can-eat spaghetti dinners for hunters staggering out twelve hours later. There are also many family camps, passed down through generations. Empty most of the year, uncles and cousins are sometimes only able to meet and get acquainted here on first

61

Monday. In towns where merchants normally close every evening of the week, grocery stores and sporting goods shops stay open until midnight, while state police work overtime to bring some semblance of order to what inevitably becomes the longest-running traffic jam of the year. Annually the thirteen-day season accounts for a $100 million boost to the economy.

We are not one big happy family, but it is always very pleasant during dinner at Jenny's on Sunday evening, although perhaps a bit reserved. Everyone is trying too hard to be gracious, passing plates heaped with vegetables and meats, telling antiseptic jokes at which we all laugh politely. The Browns are obviously not the only blacks in the woods, but they are certainly alone here in these lily-white parts. A young man from down the road once summed up the attitudes about blacks here in the outback. He told me that black people were dirty, dumb, and destructive. "They've ruined the cities, and pretty soon they'll come up here and make a mess of the woods." I asked how many blacks attended his high school. He shrugged. "I never met a nigger in my life."

Mr. Brown is a big man with broad shoulders, gray hair, and an air of authority as the ranking elder. Although he is seventy-eight and Uncle Shorty is seventy-four, they both have killed a buck as recently as the year before last. At dinner, Brown often reminds us how difficult it was deer hunting when he was a boy.

Two centuries ago, deer were plentiful in Pennsylvania, as were buffalo and elk, but after many years of abuse by settlers clearing land to plow and plant and hunters selling meat and hides, the deer herd was nearly exterminated. As a last-ditch effort, the

Pennsylvania Game Commission made it illegal to shoot deer for market, hunt deer with dogs, or kill a deer at salt licks. Game refuges were also established, and the commission began releasing deer into remote mountain regions. In 1907, the shooting of antlerless deer was outlawed. From then on, the number of deer in Pennsylvania began to increase rapidly. In 1915, hunters took 1,200 deer. Five years later, at about the same time Mr. Brown was learning to hunt, Pennsylvanians harvested 3,000 buck. Last year nearly 200,000 whitetails were killed in Pennsylvania, more than in any other state except Texas, six times Pennsylvania's size. In comparison, 2,840 deer were taken in Connecticut.

Although technically successful, the game commission's policies have caused new and serious problems. Pennsylvania's deer herd has become much too large for the area in which it feeds, and, consequently, deer are considerably smaller than the original whitetail. Farmers also lose millions of dollars annually in crops destroyed by hungry, desperate deer. More than 25,000 are mutilated on the highways. The situation is similar in other states, especially New York and Michigan, third and fourth in the harvest count. Those opposed to reducing Pennsylvania's deer herd by hunting (or any other reasonable method)—and many people are—need only to hike into the mountains in early April, as melting snow uncovers the rotting carcasses of deer that have starved to death. They will soon change their minds.

I am always somewhat amazed at the rampant imagination of the nonhunter describing the annihilation of the defenseless whitetail. Contrary to popular belief, deer do not line up outside the hunting camp, take a number, and calmly wait their turn to be shot.

For one thing, deer are extremely cagey. As soon as the shooting starts first Monday, bucks automatically tuck their heads down and conceal themselves within the herd so that the hunter has a difficult time seeing "bone." Does will also engineer diversions, moving en masse in one direction, allowing a buck to slip silently past the hunter in the other.

Although deer are color blind, they have super-sensitive eyesight when it comes to detecting motion. Scratch your nose or wiggle your fingers, and, chances are, a deer fifty yards away will see it and run. But more than on its eyesight or superior hearing, a deer relies primarily on its ability to sniff out an enemy in order to survive.

Conservation officers in Michigan once fenced off a square mile of typical deer country, into which they released thirty-nine deer, including nine bucks. From that point, it took more than four days before the six experienced hunters assigned to the project even saw a buck, and required an average of fifty-one hours hunting for each buck taken.

In the Academy Award–winning film, *The Deer Hunter*, Robert DeNiro stalks a deer up a mountain, supposedly in western Pennsylvania, but actually somewhere in the Cascades in Washington. He finally sees the beast, sporting a treelike rack, standing majestically on a rocky plateau at the very top of the slope, framed against the sky. DeNiro stoops down, steadies himself on one knee, carefully measures the animal through the cross hairs, and finally shoots. From an experienced deer hunter's point of view, the scene is unlikely.

Not only would a buck probably not permit itself to be caught, unconcealed, but instead of stalking, hunters will usually select a high spot with a good view of trail crossings and feeding areas and wait. Chances are, they'll see "bone" sooner or later. During the first few days, the many hunters in the woods will keep the deer moving, but during the latter part of the season, the few remaining hunters will station themselves at opposite ends of the woods, and then take turns "driving" the deer ahead of them, toward the waiting group. Some good hunters do try stalking, like DeNiro, especially in new snow, when footprints are clear (a doe print is pointed, a buck rounder). But it takes a geat deal of time, patience, and most of all, luck, to be successful. In deer hunting, "success" means earning a clean shot. Hunters should not shoot unless reasonably certain they can kill instantly. Many "purists" refuse to go into the woods with the sophisticated weapons available today, preferring bow and arrow or flintlock rifles (accounting for about twelve thousand deer killed). Handguns are also becoming more popular. A woman once emerged from under a snow-covered army blanket as I walked up the trail one morning before sunrise, cocking a .44 Magnum. "I've been here all night," she hissed. "Now get the hell out of my spot."

Considering all the guns and people in the woods, there are surprisingly few fatalities. Two people were killed and six others were wounded by stray bullets during first Monday in 1982, and in all of Pennsylvania, ten people died in 1983 in accidents related to hunting. According to the Pennsylvania Game Commission, the rate of hunting accidents has decreased from about forty-two per hundred thousand hunters in 1969 to fifteen per hundred thousand in 1980. The commission attributes much of its improvement to the mandatory hunter education law requiring first-time hunters under sixteen to take a specially designed safety course. A more recent law, also very helpful, requires deer hunters to wear a minimum of one hundred square inches of blaze orange.

At about 10:00 P.M. the night before first Monday, we all pile into Larry's Blazer and start up the road. Immediately, we roll down the windows and turn on the spotlight. The bright yellow beam slashes through the darkness like a laser.

I have always been thrilled by the ritual of spot-lighting and the excitement that bubbles through us at the sight of herds of thirty or forty deer, down from the tree line to feed, and by the thick syrup of antic-ipation we all share for tomorrow's hunt. The antic-ipation continues to intensify as the night passes—no one sleeps too well before first Monday—and reaches a heightened pitch as we stumble out of bed, pull on layers of long johns, load up our rifles, and trudge up the steep hill and through the darkness to our chosen spot in the woods.

Hours later, dawn comes creeping up like a cloudy mirage, and I awaken into another world. First the chipmunks, their heads popping out of tiny dens like jacks-in-the-box, cast an obligatory but careless glance in all directions. They always remind me of wind-up toys, scurrying here and there, but never quite getting anything done. But the squirrels are constantly working. From the first bare reflection of light, to the full burst of daybreak, they transport nuts, seeds, and other provisions up into their trees. Meanwhile, rabbits hop in and out of the underbrush, always dashing. As I watch, the world passes before me like one of those foggy fairy tales of my youth, where animals act like humans and people don't exist.

If I remain stark still and only slightly breathing, the animals don't pay much attention. They don't come too close, but they don't avoid me either. It is always unreal and mystical here in the lifting darkness. The continuous cold weighs down my eyelids, and the sheer beauty of the wilderness in winter, with the sculptured skeleton of trees black against the pure white of the snow, and the breeze playing a faint lullaby with the leaves, is like a dream itself.

For some reason, deer do not sense danger from above, which is why so many hunters will spend their precious autumn hours building tree stands. I once looked down from a tree I had clumsily climbed in the predawn darkness at a doe and her two fawns feeding directly below me. It was a magical sight, and I was able to watch a long time without being discovered. But it is difficult and uncomfortable to stay anchored in a tree with a rifle and fifteen pounds of clothes, poised and ready to aim and fire, yet all the while unmoving. Not too long after the mama deer and her fawns wandered away in the woods, I slipped and fell twenty feet. First Monday ended for me that year with a concussion.

That was the same season in which Larry's son, Todd, sixteen, downed his first buck, a large seven-pointer. It happened early in the morning, but by the time he gutted the deer and dragged it out of the woods, it was nearly noon. Larry was waiting. Todd's eyes grew rounder and his slender face beamed with pride as he and his father hoisted the big buck and hung it from the ceiling of Jenny's front porch. Through the day and early evening, hunters cruise the countryside to admire all the deer taken first Monday. Although hardly necessary, Todd stood guard, informing everyone with a raised forefinger:

"One shot." Larry later snapped a picture of his son with the buck. He has a similar photo of himself with his own first kill, taken by his father, twenty-five years before.

It would be naive to assume that most (or any) hunters are in the woods first Monday because of some sort of moral obligation to deer or the over-browsed range. Obviously, they participate for more personal reasons, beginning with the notion of providing meat for their families, as did their fathers and grandfathers before them. But there's more to it than that. There is something very special, primeval, and intoxicating about men coming together to perform the ancient act of hunting. To many men it is far more arousing and considerably more spiritually rewarding than the jovial backslapping good cheer of the Sunday afternoon softball game or the Tuesday night bowling league. More than anything, Larry and many of his contemporaries from Munhall, Pennsylvania, and all over the country, hunt deer because of the seed planted in them by their fathers and elders years ago.

In many blue-collar families first Monday is a benchmark in a boy's life, similar to a bar mitzvah, a rite of passage on a long and seemingly uphill road toward manhood. At practically no other time of the year, except to a limited extent for fishing season (backpacking is generally not part of the work-ingman's culture), do fathers and sons spend entire days together, without the pressures and distractions of day-to-day life. Sharing the mystery and thrill of the hunt, their relationship can solidify in the back-woods, and mature in those unspoken ways unattainable at home. "Being in the woods first Monday with my father, who died last year, and now with my son," says Larry, "makes me part of something that started before I was born and will continue long after I die."

Paul Bunyan
Cherry Tree Joe
Johnny Appleseed
George Washington Sears
and the Ever-Popular
Mike Fink

PROBABLY more great American heroes have been born, bred, or conjured up in the wilds of western Pennsylvania than anywhere else in the nation. The exploits of Jim Bridger and Jeremiah Johnson in Wyoming and Montana are formidable, but tame in the face of the legends of Cherry Tree Joe McCreery and the King of the Keelboatmen, Mike Fink.

Weaned on the rivers of western Pennsylvania, Fink was known and respected from the headwaters of the Ohio to the mouth of the Mississippi. Even President Abraham Lincoln followed his career with uncommon zeal. Lincoln was especially tickled by how Fink and his keelboating cronies pledged their undying friendship. After drinking and celebrating all night, they'd stagger onto Main Street at dawn, load up their rifles, pace off seventy yards, then shoot cups of whiskey off one another's heads.

Fink was a contemporary of Daniel Boone, but so great was the difference in their daring accomplishments that, as observed in the *New York Times* in a review of a biography of Fink written by a professor at the University of Chicago in 1936, "beside Mike's raw-fisted escapades and forthrightness, Boone's slyest, most sportive venture was but a frolic of Little Lord Fauntleroy."

Oldtimers say that Cherry Tree Joe McCreery would tie a raft to each foot and skate down the Allegheny River. He could go a lot faster when the river was frozen. At his cabin, located on the Creek Without End near the town of Cherry Tree in Indiana County, Joe kept a full-grown moose in his barn for milking, and he had a panther for a house pet. Joe's wife cooked in a frying pan so large she needed a whole side of bacon just to grease it. It took a fifty-pound sack of flour and a barrel of syrup each morning to satisfy Joe's gnawing hunger for flapjacks.

Legend aside, Joe was actually a strong, skilled lumberman, the first to guide a raft of logs down the dangerous part of the West Branch of the Susquehanna River. He became a Civil War hero at age fifty-six—a member of Pennsylvania's famous sharpshooting Bucktail Regiment—who lost a leg at Gettysburg, but steadfastly continued fighting another year until he was certain the South was whipped. Although McCreery never gained the national reputation he deserved as Cherry Tree Joe, he was the inspiration behind the work of an enterprising Minnesota advertising executive, who created a series of

71

fantastic tales about the exploits of a mythical lumberjack giant called Paul Bunyan.

Incidentally, one of Cherry Tree Joe's best friends, John Chapman, planted his first apple orchard along Brokenstraw Creek in Warren County in the Allegheny National Forest, and eventually became even more famous than Bunyan, as the legendary symbol of fruit and good cheer, Johnny Appleseed.

The saga of Long John Weakland begins a few miles down the road from Cherry Tree in Carrolltown, Indiana County. Although he was a huge man, with square shoulders, sledgehammer arms, and two black brushes for brows over cold gray eyes, Weakland was deeply religious, devoted to Prince Demetrius Gallitzin, a Russian nobleman turned wilderness priest, who called himself Father Augustine Smith. So strict and straitlaced a clergyman was Smith-Gallitzin that men and women were not permitted to sit on the same side of the aisle at his church.

But when a disgruntled congregation finally confronted him one morning outside the chapel, Long John Weakland suddenly stepped out of the shadowed forest and pulled an oaken fence rail up out of the ground with his right arm.

"If anybody dares lay hands on the annointed of the Lord, let him beware," Weakland announced. "For as sure as I live, I'll crush his skull."

Long John Weakland was so massive in size and dead set in manner that most people disappeared even before his short speech ended.

When Long John died in 1854 at age ninety-six, he was originally buried at St. Augustine's Church, but his body was exhumed several years later for reburial near Carrolltown at St. Joseph's Mission Church.

When his grave was reopened, Long John's body was obviously decomposed—all except his right arm. "When Mr. Weakland's body was being removed from the grave in which it had first reposed," wrote Sister Martini in *The History of St. Augustine Parish,* published in 1922, "his hand and arm were found to be incorrupted."

Perhaps the most important and impressive of the mountain men of Penn's Woods West was an explorer, conservationist, and writer of remarkable prose whose words and observations have become the bible of the "grand army of the outers" he served.

As a teenager, George Washington Sears, who took the name of his Indian tutor, Nessmuk, shipped out of New Bedford, Massachusetts, on a whaling vessel bound for the South Pacific. This was the same year and the same port from which Herman Melville departed on the voyage that was to lead to the writing of *Moby Dick.*

An incurable wanderer, Nessmuk constantly left his tiny cabin in Pennsylvania's massive Grand Canyon, where he supported himself and financed his adventures working as a cobbler, in search of new lands and experiences about which to write. He traveled for three summers through the malaria-infested swamps of the Florida Everglades studying insects and alligators, followed by winters in the subzero icebox of northern Ontario, learning all he could about hunting and trapping from the half-caste French and Indian inhabitants. Later, he joined Cherry Tree Joe McCreery in the Bucktail Regiment and fought in the Civil War.

In all of his hundreds of articles and in all his journals, Nessmuk preached to his readers to travel as light as possible, with little more than a rifle,

73

compass, and bedroll. His objective was to show out-
doorsmen "how to smooth it rather than rough it" in
the wilderness. Nessmuk, incidentally, was barely
five feet tall. He weighed 112 pounds.

For his remarkable ten-year exploration of the
Adirondack Mountains, a project initiated when he
was fifty-one years old, Nessmuk designed and built
a series of featherweight cedar canoes, which grew
lighter with each modification and each subsequent
voyage from the *Nessmuk* (17¾ pounds) down to the
Hairy Gamp a few years later (10½ pounds), still
available for inspection in the Adirondack Museum
at Blue Mountain Lake, New York.

His explorations and his compulsion to design and
build stronger and lighter canoes continued. He
returned to Florida to chart the alligator-infested
bayous and test the rough surf of the Keys in his
masterpiece, the *Rushton*, which weighed less than
ten pounds. In comparison, the lightest canoes today,
made with far superior aluminum and fiberglass
materials, weigh considerably more and cost a minimum of a thousand dollars. Even the most daring
seaman would hesitate to explore the surf of the
Florida Keys in any canoe, let alone a fragile wooden
one, and especially for nearly two years straight, as
did Nessmuk, when he was sixty-five years old.

Today, there are many monuments and organiza-
tions dedicated to Nessmuk, including a state park, a
mountaintop, and a lake in central Pennsylvania.
And soon after he died, the editors of *Forest and
Stream*, then the bible of outdoor journalism, called
Nessmuk the "greatest woodsman who ever wrote."

Although Nessmuk's articles, letters, and poems
appreared in many other magazines, including the
Atlantic Monthly, it was 1884 before his first book,

Woodcraft, was published. The book sold out an edition a year for the first eleven years and three more editions during the next dozen years. And even though camping conditions and equipment have changed considerably, *Woodcraft* is still popular today both in England and in the United States, especially in areas such as the Alaskan outback, where the battle for survival rages twenty-four hours a day.

In *Coming Into the Country*, his fine book about Alaska, author John McPhee explains why Nessmuk's words and observations have remained viable after a century in which our society has faced radical and unprecedented change. Nessmuk's *Woodcraft*, observes McPhee, "is written with so much wisdom, wit and insight that it makes Henry David Thoreau seem humorless, alien and French."

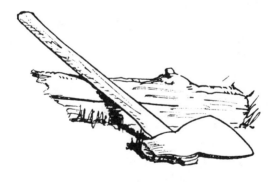

Mountain Man McCool

I reached for McCool's Workingman's Tobacco pouch on the dashboard, dug out a ragged chaw, and stuffed it into my mouth. I uncorked the fifth of George Dickel sourmash we had been sharing and took a swig, pouring it down through the tobacco. The bottle was hot from sitting in the sun. The whiskey, mixed with bits of tobacco, tore down my throat like a tornado.

McCool pointed straight ahead through the windshield toward a hulking formation of gray sandstone soaked with dark green moss and announced that this was the spot where he had captured a gigantic rattlesnake the spring before last. "Came out from behind them big rocks over there and tore 'crost the road. You shoulda seen that slitherin' sonofabitch; it was nearly five feet long."

Like any good woodsman, Harry McCool's memory for rocks, stumps, trees, and the events surrounding them is uncanny. He knows where he's caught hundreds of rattlesnakes over the years and can lead you back through half a lifetime of hunting to the exact point on which he spotted, tracked, and subsequently shot nearly all of his whitetail deer. He can remember the time of day, the color of the sky, the direction in which the wind was blowing the moment he fired. Invariably, he will know the size of the rack to the point (antlers are counted by the tips or sharp ends), the weight of the deer almost to the pound, and the age of the animal judging from its teeth. He will be even more precise when it comes to rattlers.

McCool was wearing what he always wears: a fringed buckskin shirt, a battered, sweat-stained Stetson with a russet rattlesnake skin band, black hightop combat boots, and a homemade knife with an elkhorn handle in a sheath on his belt. That afternoon he had added a bulky necklace, made from a rattlesnake skeleton, to his wardrobe.

"Them bones come apart in sections," he said. "I scrubbed them with a toothbrush, bleached them with Clorox, then strung 'em all together with fishing line." Steering the truck with one hand, he lifted the necklace off and slipped it over my head. Two bones, about three inches long with nodules at one end, hung down from the necklace as pendants.

"What are these?"

"Them's coonrackers." McCool's smokey voice conjures up visions of wagon wheels, whitewater, coyotes, and coonskin caps.

"What?"

He ran a hand through his scraggly beard, spat a wad of tobacco juice out the window. His whole face curled up and he started to snicker. "That's what you wish you had."

"I don't even know what they are."

Now he was laughing, and when I insisted I didn't know what he was talking about, he got to laughing even harder. McCool laughs as if the whole world is laughing with him. I couldn't help feeling stupid and ridiculous, watching him jump and shake.

"C'mon McCool, what's so damn funny?"

"It's a penis bone. Special to coons."

"How so?"

Because of the bone, McCool informed me, raccoons are in a permanent state of erection.

McCool downshifted into second gear as we shot over a creek bed and bounced up the bank. A clear stream paralleled the rolling dusty road for a hundred yards or so. The water was black in the shade, but the smooth stones underneath the water glowed golden green in the places where the sunlight bled through the trees. McCool pointed to a couple of deep pools where a fella might scare up a fish or two, were he so inclined. He spaced his big forefinger and thumb five inches apart to indicate size and smacked his lips, allowing that the fish here would probably be native brookies. The state-stocked trout tasted like soap. As if to wash out the memory of the taste, he reached for the whiskey. I could see the bottom of the bottle bubble as he poured the sour-mash down like soda pop.

We were following a lumpy, long-abandoned logging road cut along a ridge through typical northwestern Pennsylvania terrain, bordering the Allegheny National Forest, a half million acres of forest and streams just a hundred miles north of Pittsburgh. Not too far south of here the official weather forecast for the final six weeks of winter has been proclaimed each February 2 since 1887 by the world-renowned Punxsutawney groundhog.

There are few big mountains in this part of Pennsylvania and hardly any flatlands. Each county is comprised of hundreds of hills, high and higher, prickled with ash and oak and pine, and pressed up against one another. From the air, the terrain resembles a herd of massing buffalo. The ridge we were on fell sharply down to the right and climbed gradually to the left, giving us the illusion of riding on a narrow mountain switchback. The large moss-covered boulders, rusted by centuries of rain washing down the hillside clay, added to the illusion, while the ground was made mystical by the delicate shafts of fern, sprouting like feathers from the moist ground.

Although McCool had slowed the truck down somewhat, each time we hit a bump or dip in the road, his head banged the roof. Not that this affected him. At six foot two and 235 pounds, with a barrel chest and bulging arms, Harry McCool may well be one of the most indestructible creatures on earth — America's answer to Godzilla. I've seen him work in these woods, cutting timber for twelve hours straight, then go home and plow his fields. He squeezes the last glimmer of light out of the day before tramping into his garage to fix cars. Right now, McCool drives a perfectly tuned rust-free Chevy pickup, purchased new by his father in 1952.

I reached over, grabbed the bottle, and took another belt of Dickel. McCool removed his Stetson and set it down on the dashboard. His long hair and his bristly unkempt bush of a mustache and beard were plastered down against his chin and around his bull neck. It was stinking hot in the truck with the ninety-degree heat beating down on the roof and the two of us perspiring like crazy. The straight sour-mash, mixed with the tobacco, made it seem even hotter. But neither of us seemed to mind.

It was the middle of the summer, and we had spent

most of the afternoon scanning the side of the road for rattlers, wriggling or resting in the underbrush, or sunning themselves lazily on rocks. Actually, we weren't *really* rattlesnake hunting, not officially and formally anyway. We lacked the paraphernalia—the snakebite kit, the canvas sack, the pinning fork— although I guess if we would have come upon one of those nasty critters, McCool might have barehanded it, tied it into a knot, and tossed it into the back of the truck for later. The hunting was simply something to say we were doing while we involved ourselves in the much more serious tasks of chewing and drinking.

Besides, this was hardly the perfect time to hunt rattlers; it was too goddamn hot for the goddamn rattlers to be out, McCool said. Buzztails prefer less sunny and more sultry summer days. But as he took one more hit of Dickel, McCool speculated that the rattlers were a damn sight smarter than we were, hiding somewhere in the shade, while we rode around cooking in the heat. "Although when you come right down to it, they couldn't actually be feelin' as good as us, them poor sonsabitches."

I told McCool that I had never been on a rat- tlesnake hunt before, although I had experienced some pretty good drunks in my day, and this was stacking up to be one of the best. But now without any rattlers to show for our trouble, I sort of felt as if I had missed out on something. I hadn't looked a buzztail close up in the eye, listened to the anger of its rattle, watched it flex and coil and strike. Although I was halfway joking, I guess I got carried away with the sound of my own words and the brave picture of myself I was painting. In truth, I was relieved to have escaped having to face down a rattler. I knew McCool would have taken care of me, if necessary, but after all, I was only a flatlander. God knows what I might have blundered into. But to Harry McCool and others of his breed, rattlers are not a joking matter. Without another word, McCool made a quick U-turn and caromed down the narrow roadway at top speed. "What the hell are you doing?" I wanted to know. But McCool was too busy driving to answer.

In just a few minutes we pulled up to an old corrugated-metal building near the headquarters of Clear Creek State Park across the river from the Allegheny National Forest, where McCool works as a resident roadbuilder and woodsman. Without a word, he jumped out of the truck. For a second, I watched him go. McCool moves with the blind bulldozing confidence of a grizzly bear; he never seems to look where he's going; he walks as if he has a vision of his destination rather than a view of it.

When I finally followed him inside, he was already across the room. There was a refrigerator in the corner. He yanked open the freezer compartment and pulled out an old blue-burned cast-iron frying pan and quickly handed it to me. I took it without thinking—I couldn't imagine what he had in mind—and looked down. Inside the frying pan was a rattle-snake, leering up at me—coiled in striking position.

For an instant, I stopped breathing. Face-to-face with a rattler, I honestly feared that my number was up. I imagined the searing inevitability of pain as its tendrils cut into me.

Of course, nothing happened; the rattler did not move, regarding me silently with menacing, beady eyes. There was a familiar white fuzz on its delicately arched head. I reached out and touched it. Its skin was cold and hard. McCool's rattlesnake was frozen solid.

81

McCool, all the while, had been snickering. McCool has this way of tossing his head and chuckling, beaming from one whole side of his face. The other side is always balled up with tobacco. When he gets like this, he looks gigantic, ferocious, and completely ridiculous, sort of a cross between Gabby Hayes and Baby Snooks, with a one-sided case of the mumps. When I looked at him, I started laughing. Once I started, I couldn't stop.

The full scope of Harry McCool's universe starts and ends no more than thirty miles in any direction from Clear Creek State Park and his house a few miles away in Jefferson County. There is hardly anything McCool does not know about the people, the forest, and the tiny towns within these boundaries, and hardly anything he knows from first-hand experience about the world beyond them. Except for a single overnight excursion into Canada twenty years ago, trucking timber for a neighbor, McCool has never stepped a foot out of western Pennsylvania or ventured farther than fifty miles from his birthplace in his entire life. Neither has Mary Jane, his wife of thirty-two years, or any of their five children. Two of McCool's offspring have finished high school; Hunter, eighteen, named because of a big deer McCool downed the day he was born, will be the third. Since his father was the local schoolmaster, McCool held out longer than most of his contemporaries, making it through the eighth grade.

Although he wouldn't trade his work at Clear Creek fixing roads and cutting timber for anything other than fully subsidized retirement, McCool's salary hardly goes halfway toward paying the mortgage and all the other bills, as well as feeding the family.

Most of his children still live with him, while eldest son Vern and his wife and child live in a trailer down the road. As did his Scotch-Irish and Seneca ancestors before him, McCool relies on the fields and forests to supply much of his food, clothing, and fuel.

McCool grows his own vegetables, raises hogs, cuts wood for winter. He reserves a week of vacation each year to crawl into seemingly impenetrable patches of bramble and weeds to pick huckleberries and blackberries. Mary Jane cooks and cans them. The McCools don't do anything different during the rest of their vacation time than they do during their weeks at work. They hardly ever go into town— they never seem to go anywhere. Years ago, they used to go down to the community center to listen to some of the local boys pick and stomp, but now that "HeeHaw" is on TV, they don't even need to leave the house. The nineteen-inch color television is one of the McCools' few modern conveniences.

"That's the way it is up here," McCool once told me. "You go to school a little, you work a little, you get drunked up on Saturday nights, wreck some cars. And then you get married, get yourself a house, and settle in. I wouldn't know no other way."

McCool hunts deer, turkey, rabbit, squirrel, and an occasional groundhog for meat. In summer, there is almost always fish on the dinner table. In winter, McCool, his children, and grandchildren, wear home-made coonskin caps to keep out the cold. Slits, where the coon once had eyes, peak out above their fore-heads. McCool deplores people who hunt animals simply for the sake of the kill, and shares with many long-entrenched backwoods people a special affinity for the rattler.

"Rattlesnakes are just another goddamn creature

83

that the Good Lord put here, don't ask me why. But to go hunting for them when they're in the goddamn woods minding their own business just to play with them or kill them, ain't right. If you're gonna kill the sonofabitch, use it for something. I don't believe in wasting anything."

McCool assured me he puts "every goddamn part of the rattler to good use." He described the entire process from beginning to end in graphic backcountry detail.

"After I shoot the rattler, I lay it down on a tree stump, cut its goddamn head off, kick a hole in the mud, and bury it. Then I sharpen up my knife and skin 'em, slit 'em right through the belly from the head to the rattles. When skinning rattlers, you should always hold the head end high, pushing on its guts and working down. Otherwise, the sonofabitch is liable to shit a brown streak all over you.

"Skin 'em all the way down to the asshole, slit the tail to its rattle. You got to watch careful now, 'cause right there the sonofabitch'll shit for sure. Now peel the skin away, stretch it out on a board, tack it in place, sprinkle it with salt and alum and leave 'er set."

"How do you cook it up?"

"You boil him in water two or three hours, until the bones slip away from the meat. You put the meat in a pan with some salt and fry 'em up. Tastes something like chicken, 'cept not as good."

"And then you use the skeleton for necklaces . . ."

McCool nodded. "And I make hat bands from the hides."

"Anything else?"

"Earache medicine," McCool announced. "This comes from an Indian recipe passed down to me from my granddaddy's brother, old Billy Long, who used to hunt panther up and down the Clarion. The Indians called him Long Knife."

"How do you do that?"

"There's a layer of fat on both sides of the stomach. Before I cook the meat, I dig out the fat and save it. You get one of them critters in the summertime, and if he's lived pretty good, well, you've got yourself a nice supply down there. To render the earache medicine, you put the fat in a frying pan and put on a little heat. Not much, just a little. Pretty soon, the oil begins to come out of the fat, and you pour it off into a little container. I don't get the earache much, but when I do I pour a few drops of that stuff in there and she's cleared up in no time."

I asked McCool if there were other remedies he could recommend.

"In summertime when it's real hot and sticky, I might get galled between the legs. The Indians used to take a handful of crude oil directly from the ground and smear it on them. When I can't find crude, I take some grease from my grease gun, squirt a little bit out, and rub it on where she's chafed. That cup grease is about as pure as any petroleum jelly."

Later, when we stopped at a gas station down the road, I saw an old man accidentally slam the door of his pickup on his finger. Although it was bleeding only slightly, the finger seemed a mess. It swelled up immediately to about twice its normal size and started to turn red and blue.

The gas station attendant dug a bottle of clear liquid out of his toolbox, soaked some cotton in it, and dabbed it over the old man's finger. In no more than ten minutes, the swelling had nearly disappeared, and the finger was no longer discolored. I was astounded, but the attendant shrugged it off. "Just something my grandfather taught me."

"Some sort of home brew?"

"No," he said, "I bought it."

"At the drugstore?"

He smiled. "More'n likely the hardware store."

"The hardware store? What the hell is it?"

"Straight turpentine."

McCool's barn is crammed with all sorts of tools and equipment, ratty old furniture in need of repair, a rambling collection of parts from an array of dismantled vehicles, license plates from every state in the Union—some predating the Depression, and an old patched-up Holex motorcycle, a make that hasn't been manufactured for three decades. McCool's dream is to one day buy himself a Harley Davidson "hog," the Cadillac of two-wheel travel, but at this particular time, "with only ten cents in my pocket and nothin' in the bank," he'll be glad to settle for a genuine Nazi combat helmet, if he can ever pick one up for the right price. As a makeshift mechanic and master scavenger, almost all of his tools, furniture, gadgets, and gizmos have been liberated from the junk heap at one time or another, and restored.

It is a spacious affair, designed and constructed three summers ago by McCool and his sons, set into the middle of a graveled drive with two big double doors—front and back—permitting a vehicle as large as a flatbed truck to drive through the barn and down to the outbuildings, where the hogs and goats are penned. A red, white, and blue target, reinforced by three bales of hay, stands between the barns and the pens. During the course of a long day, young Hunter will periodically drop whatever else he is doing, take out his Bear compound bow, walk down the drive to the main road—and shoot at the target straight through the barn, just to make sure he can split the bull's-eye forty yards. McCool will also periodically take a potshot with the .44 Magnum revolver he keeps loaded in the glove compartment of his pickup, just to keep his shooting eye sharpened up. It's a real cannon, the kind Clint Eastwood uses in all of his *Dirty Harry* films. One bullet could rip off the top of an elephant's head, reduce a cement block to a heap of dust. "She'll go off if you breathe too hard," McCool assured me.

Most nights McCool sleeps right out here on a striped, lumpy mattress, dropped onto the rusty skeleton of an old hospital bed. There are neither sheets on the bed nor heat in the barn. I asked him once if he ever got cold in the dead of winter. He said he was generally OK under eight blankets, but had yet to test his resolution past twenty below. Except to eat or watch TV, he hardly ever goes into the main house. In fact, his real "home" is up in the large loft above the barn, with most of his treasured possessions.

The room is filled with odd, gnarled formations of roots, long-outdated calendars, yellowed pinups of sparsely clad bathing beauties, portraits and photos of almost all of his ancestors going back four generations (including Billy Long and granddaddy McCool who fought for the North at Gettysburg), antique tools, musical instruments, presidential campaign buttons and posters dating back to 1948, Indian relics, pitchforks, plows—and guns. There are guns leaning in dusty corners, guns on the bed, guns in every chair, under every table, hanging on the walls. The whole place reminds me of one of those outlaw hideouts in the Old West; at any minute the Dalton brothers could burst through the door and blast us all to smithereens.

McCool owns an original Pennsylvania long rifle dating back to the eighteenth century, the kind Dan'l Boone used (and in perfect shooting condition), an authentic flintlock pistol, a German Luger with an intricately carved ivory handle, a revolver originally used by the U.S. Cavalry during the Civil War, a .30–.40 Krag made in Austria-Hungary before the turn of the century, and a Colt .45 six-shooter, the gun that helped tame the Old West. McCool also owns and proudly displays a vast array of artillery ammunition—live—used by the Allies during World War II. But his favorite gun is an old Hopkins and Allen .22. "My dad and me rode into town in a horse and buggy one morning and traded tobacco wrappers for it," he told me.

"What happens if gun control laws are instituted? Would you give up your guns when they came to get them?"

McCool reached for the Dickel and hoisted it to his lips, burying the neck of the bottle in the briar of his beard. Then he dug some tobacco out of his gums with a forefinger. "I'll be very cordial."

"And then what?"

"I'll go inside and get out all my guns and load 'em up," McCool paused, raised a scraggy eyebrow, winked, and nodded. "And then," he said quietly, "I'd tell 'em to come and get 'em."

The loft is the highest point of the property, and a trapdoor down at the far end overlooks most of McCool's land. After work and on weekends, McCool will entertain himself right here, resting in an old rickety rocking chair with the trapdoor swung wide open, his mandolin cradled in his lap, picking and singing. Sometimes Vern will wander in from next door carrying his five-string banjo, while Sheila strums her guitar. McCool's eyes dance and his ample jaws quiver to the beat of "Turkey in the Straw" or "Lucille." His twangy, toothless voice captures the poor sorrowful sound of the backwoods farmer, left alone with "four hungry children and a crop in the field" by a thankless woman. McCool sings the words as if he feels the pain.

Sometimes McCool is willing to go into the nearest town, fifteen miles down the road, to perform at the Fourth of July festivities in return for a couple of bottles of good Canadian whiskey. "Beer gets awfully ordinary week after week."

But nearly always he is happiest right here. A translucent scrim of contentment slightly softens the wild spark in the lightning blue eyes as he sits in the throne of his loft and watches over his golden fields and the rich, lush woods behind them.

Although he has actually owned this property for only ten years, the McCools have long been rooted here. The house was built in 1928 by his mother's family, mostly carpenters, on land originally owned generations ago by the McCool clan and subsequently sold. "In 1941 my dad bought some of the property back, cleared a piece of ground, and built a place right up above here." He pointed in a northerly direction. "You can't see through the trees, but it's awful close. My brother lives in that same house today. In fact, most of my family, alive or dead, ain't no more than five miles away from this here spot."

Ten years ago, McCool purchased the remaining twenty-eight-acre plot, the house included. When Vern married, McCool presented him with three acres up the road. "He set a trailer on there, then built him a house around it. I don't tell my kids where to go or what to do; if they want to leave home, more power to them. But they're welcome to stay right here if they can find work."

"What was the first job you ever had?"

"Cuttin' logs down in Gumtown, about two mile north of Kittanning. Used a crosscut saw. I'd drive out to Corsica each day and pick up my buddy, Blaine Moore. We always called him Nig. We'd fly down that goddamn road in his Studebaker Land Cruiser and be there in an hour. The only times we was ever late was when he would get behind a state cop or when it was rainin'. The roads in the rain was solid mud. Half the time, you'd end up walkin'.

"We'd work all day in the goddamn rain—didn't ever seem to get the flu—then go into town and get a fifth of Seagram's Seven and some 7-Up, and come home soaked to the ass. That was the first job I ever had. Got a dollar an hour, a lot more, by Jesus, than I do right now." McCool is on call day and night at Clear Creek for road repairs, snow plowing, firefighting, and all other emergencies. He makes about sixteen thousand dollars a year.

"When I was a kid, things was pretty damn tough up here; a fella didn't have much. We had enough clothes to get by with, and although we didn't eat that good, we always had somethin'. I was born during the Depression in '33. My dad would teach school and run up a big bill at the general store to feed us through the winter. And then he'd work all summer for the gas company, mowing grass with a damn old sickle to get his bill paid up. All my dad ever done in his life is work, work, work.

"The family never had a whole hell of a lot, but

90

growin' up around here was good. Some Saturdays I'd ride to town with my dad in the front seat of his old Model A and then follow my mom around the general store. Never went to town too goddamn much as I got older, though. Got so I hated it. Still do. Sometimes they made me go, but after a while I flat out refused. But my mother never failed to bring me home a pocketknife.

"We done a lot of fishin' back then. We done so much fishin' we wore a path smooth as glass running down through the woods from our house to the creek with our bare feet. Our feet always got good and calloused in the summer."

McCool said that when his daddy first started teaching he made five hundred dollars a year, and that the most he ever earned was back in 1956, his last year, when he got thirty-four hundred dollars. "But he taught the whole neighborhood, all the people that's growed up here now. My dad was dedicated. He used to wade through the snow up to his ass to get to that damn country school morning after morning in the dark of the winter."

"And you went with him?"

McCool nodded, maintaining a slow, deadpan rhythm as he rocked in his chair and looked out over his sun-soaked land. "My dad taught me four or five grades of my schoolin'."

He blinked and sat up, as if abruptly awakened. Then he sighed. Much of the harshness seemed to drain from his wrecked up face. Yesterday's child lurked in his eyes and in his suddenly soft voice behind his bramble beard. "That was a one-room schoolhouse with a coat room out back and big windows up one wall in the main room to let in the light. There was a blackboard covering the entire back

91

wall. The teacher's desk and chair were in front of maybe forty seats."

"How did your father teach the different grades?"

"By going right up through, morning and afternoon, from first to eighth in order—arithmetic, English, spelling, geography—till all grades were taught. I'll tell you," McCool cocked his finger, then paused to pluck at his old mandolin still cradled in his large lap. The instrument, with a picture of the Indian chief Pontiac tattooed on it, had been purchased by his uncle at the 1939 New York World's Fair. "If any of them little bastards had his wits about him, he could take in an awful lot just by listening to what was going on with the older kids in the other grades."

"Sounds like a good setup."

"It was a hell of a good setup. It was the ruination of the goddamn country when they took all those one-room schoolhouses out. Yeah, it was. You'd study hard all morning 'cause there wasn't nowhere you could go and hide and screw off. At noon, you'd eat your dinner and gather around an old potbelly stove to get warm. It was nice. There was a coal house right out back, and my dad would keep the stove all fired up."

"If you did wrong, what would your dad do to correct you?"

"In school, he'd sometimes take kids out into the cloakroom and give them a scutchin'. If I acted up, I'd get treated no different than the next guy. But I'll tell you, he didn't often do it. He was the kind of guy who could actually talk you out of doing bad."

"Your brothers and sisters were in school with you?"

"Quite a few of them were in the same room."

"That must have been pretty nice."

McCool paused, squinting and looking out over an ocean of space and time. The day was coming to an end. Shadows of dusk were scaling the faraway hills. Golden embers of a sinking sun dripped through the treetops like honey. "That was the best time of a fella's life," he said.

You go about a quarter mile down the graveled drive behind the barn to Lake Long Knife, three acres of sparkling blue water, mossy green around the edges. McCool created this haven one weekend a few years ago with a borrowed bulldozer. "Just a place for the old folks to get their feet wet and the kids to splash around in." A few summers back, McCool and his sons added a tiny log cabin the size of a four-man tent along with a shed and a few picnic tables.

McCool drove right into the water and stopped the truck. We both bailed out. After a thorough soaking, we took off our clothes.

Although the water was a cool, comfortable awning from the hot sun, the sandy bottom was spinning like a saucer every time I opened my eyes. Even when I closed my eyes, the world lurched and roared. I felt awful. I had drunk down much more Dickel than I was used to and, over the course of the day, had accidentally ingested about half of the tobacco I had tried to chew. Being a full-fledged western Pennsylvania mountain man was much more difficult than I had initially envisioned. I crawled to shore and plopped under a tree on my back.

Stripped of his sweaty Stetson, buckskins, and boots, McCool is a pale blur of the original mountain man, but in the water he plunged, growled, snorted, and kicked like a bear. I watched with amazement as

93

he dived again and again, trying to spear tiny fish on the sandy bottom with his fingers. I was continually awed by his energy and endurance. He spotted the Dickel where I had dropped it in the mud, went after it, tipped the bottle upside down, and gulped until the whiskey was all gone. Then he turned and looked at me, seriousness in his eyes. "My sister died this morning," he said abruptly.

"What?"

He shook his head back and forth. "The goddamn cancer just ate her away."

I wasn't certain I had heard him right. "Today?"

He nodded. "'Bout an hour before you arrived."

"But why didn't you tell me? We could have gone rattlesnake hunting some other time."

"It wouldn't have done her no good. Besides, I promised."

"I would have understood."

"A promise is a promise."

"McCool," I said, "you're something, you know that? You really are something."

"I'm tough," he agreed.

"The toughest man I've ever known."

McCool was smiling again. He tossed his head to one side, shrugged and chuckled, as he heaved himself up and out of the water like a mountain flexing its muscles. "Brother," he boomed, pounding his chest with his fist. "I'm the meanest hard-ass you'll ever want to meet. No one can outwork me. No one can outfight me. Ain't no man that scares me."

McCool paused, looked across the water at me, shook himself from head to toe, then burst out laughing.

Two weeks later, McCool called me at home, collect. He said that Mary Jane had been rushed to a Pittsburgh hospital for an emergency kidney operation. He said that although she was awfully sick, the family doctor had assured him that she would be OK. Then he asked if I would help out and handle a few things for him.

The man who could face down a bear, snare a dangerous rattler with his bare hands, cut timber from early morning to late into the night, drink a fifth of sourmash and chew a pouch of tobacco without hardly blinking an eye, was much too frightened to square off against city traffic.

I have often tried to describe Harry McCool to my friends in the city. I say to them that he is strong, noble, intelligent, and sensitive, as well as wild, vulgar, and sometimes violent. I tell them to imagine a truck driver, an outlaw, a cowboy, a porcupine, and a koala bear all rolled up into one. But my portrait never quite hits home. McCool and his friends and relatives, backwoodsmen all their lives, are much too isolated, too disconnected from the rhythm and reality of metropolitan life for flatlanders to relate to.

The one and only way to come to know Harry McCool and to understand his overpowering effect on people is to stand side by side with him. You've got to sense the animal in him, hear the soulful backwoods twang in his voice, witness the dignity and the artistry with which he works the woods, feel the sheer power of his presence when he walks through the door and fills up the room.

I respect Harry McCool for his brute strength, his knowledge of nature's ways, and I envy him for the character traits that enable him to live at peace, so satisfied with his lot in life, and so close to the roots of his culture. Although Harry McCool is not a mountain man in the strict sense of the word, he comes as close to mountain-man status as today's world will allow. Like the cowboy of the Old West, McCool is symbolic of the spirit of the settlers who first cut into the western Pennsylvania wilderness with their axes, their plows, and their dreams.

Jim Swartz

THE mystique of the rugged individualist living life in his own way and at his own uncompromising pace in the mountains was also part of Ed Peterson's fascination with the people of Penn's Woods West, although Peterson appreciated a more subtle, thoughtful approach to wilderness life.

Peterson first saw Jim Swartz, an official at Kettle Creek State Park, about fifty miles east of the Allegheny National Forest, standing at the breast of the dam, watching the swollen frothy water thunder down to the rocks below. Swartz stood motionless, erect, and serene; his reverie with the water was an act of concentrated enjoyment. At his side, in his left hand, he held a closed book. "The roar was so loud that I thought I would have to shout to get his attention," writes Peterson, "but just as I came up behind him, he turned slowly as though he had known all along that I was there. His eyes were bright black, his hair bushy and gray.

"'I was just listening to the water,' he said, by way of explanation or apology. 'I like the sound of the water.'

" 'I do, too,' I said, 'there's a lot of it.'

" 'Too much for talking,' he said. 'You're planning to camp here tonight?'

"I nodded.

" 'Let's go over to the office,' he said. He shifted the book from his left hand to his right. I tried to see the title, but could not.

"We walked silently through the hemlock woods to his office, the roar of the water growing fainter as we went. Inside he made out a camping permit. The book was lying on his desk. It was Thoreau's *Walden*. Near it was a little pile of hemlock cones. I paid him the fee of seventy-five cents.

" 'You like Thoreau?' I asked.

"For a moment I thought he resented the question. He pushed a few straggling cones into the pile. 'Yes,' he said. He looked down at the book. 'Do you?' he asked.

" 'Very much,' I said, and waited.

"In a moment he looked up from the book, his face a silhouette against the window. 'I have lived in the woods all my life,' he said, 'and so I understand them. Most people only like them, Burroughs, for instance. But Thoreau understood.' He picked up the book. 'You have to love things to understand them.'

"When he turned around, there was a little smile on his face, the smile of the weary or the sad. 'My name's Jim Swartz,' he said crisply. 'If you need anything let me know, I think you'll like Kettle Creek tonight, even if it rains.'

"When I left him he was looking out the window towards the dam."

Peterson next saw Jim Swartz the following evening. They stood together near a log, watching the water, while the dim fading sunlight touched their hair, and the wind whistled softly through the trees.

"'I knew you would like it here,' he said. 'I think I told you so.'

"'You did,' I said. 'You also mentioned Thoreau.'

"He smiled. 'Thoreau. Yes. He was more than a naturalist. He had a feeling for nature, an understanding of it. It was kind of a religion for him.'

"The whippoorwill that I heard was coming closer. It made me think of Tom's chipping sparrow, and I told Jim about how it followed Tom around.

"'Yes,' he said. 'I know the sparrow. He's been coming here for three years. Farther up the stream by the big bend, there's a towhee. It will light on your finger . . .' He paused and smiled again. 'If it trusts you.'

"'You think they can tell?' I asked.

"'I do,' he said as solemnly as if he were taking an oath. 'I think many creatures understand us better than we understand them. The dog, for instance. And the beaver. The fox you disturbed yesterday morning was not afraid of you. He understood.'

"'You were up there?' I asked.

"He did not answer. There was no sunlight in the woods now, but the reflected light from the sky seemed to catch in his bushy hair. 'There was a beaver once,' he said, and then he stopped.

"'Tell me,' I asked.

"'It had been caught in a trap. Illegally. I was a fire warden then. If I had known the man who did it . . .'

"'Hurt badly?' I asked.

"'His leg. It was a vicious wicked kind of trap.'

"'Could you do anything?' I said. 'It must have been dangerous to release a trapped beaver.'

"'I sat down near it,' he said, 'but not too near. I talked with it for a while.'

"He ran his hand through his hair, 'Be seated,' he said. 'We might as well be seated.'

"I sat down on the log beside him. Now the whip-poorwill was calling from between us and the stream.

"'You talked with the beaver,' I said. 'What did you say?'

"'Oh,' he said, 'I don't remember exactly. But I told him I was sorry. I told him I meant no harm. I explained that I wanted to help him if he would let me.'

"'You talked *words* to him?' I asked.

"'I told him we would have to go over to a tree. I would carry the trap and he would have to hobble along. I wanted the tree between us when I released the trap . . .'

"He hesitated and leaned forward, looking at the ground. 'Because sometimes when we are hurt ourselves, we want to hurt others.'

"For a minute he said nothing but he kept looking at the ground. I could hear the roar of Kettle Creek, but I do not think he heard it. He was thinking of something else. Then he straightened up.

"'I took the trap over to the tree, and he hobbled along on three legs. It was a vicious trap, and I had trouble springing it, but after a while I did, and he pulled his leg out.'

"'And then,' I said, 'he probably went off in a hurry.'

"'He just sat there for a while, and so I sat down, too, but not too near. I talked with him a little more. I told him I was sorry. I told him I thought the leg would heal. In a few minutes, I got up, and he did, too. I went one way and he went another.'

"By now it was almost dark. He was leaning forward, his elbows on his knees and his hands clasping and unclasping in front of him. I heard the whippoorwill again between us and the creek. Then another whippoorwill answered from behind us, very close, and all around were gentle night sounds of the woods.

"He got up from the log as though our talk was ended, and so I also got up.

"'Good night,' he said. His hand was hard and calloused. 'I would not have told you about it except . . .'

"I said goodnight and started up the dark path to the tenting grounds. Once I looked back. He had left the hemlock grove and was standing near the stream, in the same attitude he had been in when I first met him."

Peterson's conversation with Jim Swartz intrigued me. I decided to find out more about him.

"He was a mysterious and legendary figure in these parts," said Pat Wykoff, long-time foreman of the forest at Kettle Creek. "Jim had tuberculosis when he showed up here around 1920. No one knew where he came from, but he cured himself with rugged living. He built a cabin high up on the mountain where the air was clean and pure, and he'd never go into town unless it was absolutely necessary. He would take a bath in a barrel outside in the middle of winter, just to keep himself healthy."

Swartz was a firetowerman, according to Wykoff. "He'd sit up in the Tamarack Tower reading one book after another, and looking out into the forest for the slightest hint of smoke. He got to know the country so well, he could isolate a fire without lifting his binoculars. It was amazing," said Wykoff.

Harry Anderson, now eighty-one, but back then Supervising Forest Ranger at Kettle Creek, eventually hired Swartz as his assistant. "What I liked most about Jim was his straightforwardness and his honesty. You could depend on him. He was stubborn in an argument, but never got angry.

"He was an awful good trapper," Anderson remembers. "He cured his own hides and got top prices for them. Winter or summer, he ran around in a pair of shorts. He was never afraid of rattlers. He could talk to them easily as he could talk to me. They were his friends more than anything else.

"I always called him the Indian," Anderson continued. "And he never seemed to have no objection. To me, it looked as though Jim was leading a real Indian life."

Jim Swartz got married later in life. The woman moved to the cabin on the mountaintop with him, but disappeared sometime later. No one knows why. Swartz died in 1958—the year *Penn's Woods West* was published.

Looking for Tom Mix
Along a Road Paved With
Promises of Gold

WHEN I asked the man at the gas station
to direct me to the Paradise Gulch
Saloon, he slid out from under the car he
was working on, glanced at my motorcycle resting
beside the old-fashioned glass-domed American Oil
pump, and got to his feet.

"When?" he said.

I hesitated, looked the man up and down. He was
in his mid-fifties, short, with an overstuffed basket for
a stomach and gray bib overalls stained with grease. I
didn't know whether he was being serious or trying to
give me trouble. Sometimes, when you ride a motorcycle, people get the wrong idea about you.

"Now," I finally said.

"Well, it isn't there now," he said.

"It isn't *where* now?" I persisted.

"It isn't where it was when it was last here," he
said.

I sighed, turned away and looked down the hill

into the tired old town of Dubois, Pennsylvania, in the northwest corner of Clearfield County. Across the street and up the block from where we stood was the Flaming Earth Cafe, and although a beer would have tasted good right about then, I was holding out for the Paradise Gulch.

It had been a difficult day, the morning rainy and cold, and now the afternoon was thick with heat. Earlier, the truck winding down the narrow mountain road from Boot Jack had roared past, splattering me with mud. It had slowed down to go up the next hill, but when it came down the hill after that, I was splattered again.

I explained that I had heard about a Tom Mix festival taking place in Dubois each year to celebrate the cowboy's birthday. "I thought that the Paradise Gulch was where Tom Mix fans hang out."

Mix, incidentally, was one of the first white-hatted heroes of movie westerns, having moonlighted his first of nearly four hundred films in 1910 while working as a deputy marshall in Dewey, Oklahoma. He distinguished himself from his cowboy competitors by refusing to ever kiss a girl on film. "Rather kiss a horse," he always said.

Supposedly, the festival featured showings of Mix films, displays of Mix memorabilia, panel discussions about Tom Mix, and Mix souvenirs. The year before nearly seven thousand people attended the Tom Mix festival in Dubois, including a couple from West Germany.

"That's right," the man in the gasoline station said, "but the festival ain't until September."

"I know, but I just want to see the place."

"But it ain't real," he said. "It only exists during festival time." He chuckled and shook his head. "If we had a place like the Paradise Gulch year round, there would be nothin' left of Dubois."

The man explained that each autumn the town fathers erected the Paradise Gulch in a different spot, but that the patrons got so drunk paying homage to Mix that they'd tear the place apart long before the festival was over. The Paradise Gulch was so authentic and true to the image of the Old West, of which Mix was an integral albeit symbolic part, that some of the patrons even wore guns.

"The Paradise Gulch is a good place to go," he continued, patting his side where his six-shooter might have been and wiping his greasy hands on his knees, "if you got a grudge against somebody who's going to be there at the same time."

I thanked the man, washed up a bit, squeezed on my helmet, and headed north through Tyler, Weedville, and Caledonia toward Mix Run in Cameron County, about an hour's drive away, where Tom's grandfather had settled one hundred fifty years ago, and where the King of the Celluloid Cowboys was subsequently born. He moved to Dubois as a teenager, where he worked with his brother and sister as a stablehand.

Along the way, I would pass the ghost towns of Coalville, Glen Fisher, and Wilmer, as well as the site on which Bill Smith's Rattlesnake Zoo once stood, before old Bill caught a wet bite from a member of his friendly family of serpents and died on the spot.

This is a lovely, soothing stretch of country, with rolling meadows, fresh white church steeples, log cabins low to the ground, hills cushioned with trees, houses of natural stone. I wound my motorcycle out through all five gears. It whispered in the wind as I soared up the blacktop.

Actually, Mix never really needed to go to Hollywood to strike paydirt. According to stories and legends, there is a motherlode of treasure buried near Mix Run, beginning with $1.5 million in silver, stashed a century and a half ago by a salvage expert named Captain Blackbeard, who had raised a Spanish galleon near the port of Baltimore. While attempting to sneak the silver overland through Pennsylvania and into Canada, Blackbeard panicked, buried his treasure near the village of Gardeau in McKean County, about a day's ride from Mix Run, and fled. He was killed on a boat to England soon afterward, and the location of his treasure died with him.

At about the same time Blackbeard was hiding his silver, a man, sick and delirious, wandered into the tiny town of Hazel Hurst in McKean County and confessed to robbing a bank in nearby Emporium, making off with $60,000.

He claimed to have stuffed the money in glass jars and buried them under a large flat rock within sight of Kinsua Bridge. To this day, the rock under which the money was allegedly concealed has not been found.

But the biggest all-time payload, today worth more than $7 million, was brought into Penn's Woods West by Lieutenant Castleton of the Union Army, assigned to transport twenty-six fifty-pound bars of gold, concealed with black paint, from Wheeling, West Virginia, to Philadelphia, and to avoid detection by the Confederate Cavalry.

Castleton took the extra precaution of hiding the gold under a specially designed false bottom in his wagon, and selecting a roundabout northern route from Pittsburgh through Clarion and Ridgeway. He arrived in St. Mary's, Elk County, in June 1863, the last time in which he and his men (with one exception) were ever seen alive.

Two months later, Sergeant John Conners wandered into Lock Haven, Pennsylvania, and told a fantastic story of how the entire caravan was ambushed by highwaymen who stole the wagons. Without food or ammunition, Conners had managed to save himself only by drinking swamp water and crawling night and day through the snake-infested wilderness.

Since then, the army has conducted dozens of fruitless searches and investigations, most recently in 1941 when the Pinkerton detective agency uncovered one-half of a black-painted gold bar between Driftwood and Dent's Run. This is not much of a payload, considering all the trouble the army has gone through over the years, but it is more of a reward than I received when I rounded the last bend a few miles past Driftwood and chugged up the long hill to the site on which the town of Mix Run once stood.

All that is remaining of Tom Mix's ancestral home and the community surrounding it is a plaque, standing silent and erect like a wooden soldier on the shoulder of the lonely road:

> Tom Mix cowboy star of silent motion
> pictures was born a short distance
> from here. He served as a soldier
> in the Spanish American War, later
> becoming renowned for his wild west
> roles in cinema and circus. Mix
> died in an auto accident in Arizona
> on October 12, 1940.

The terrain flattens somewhat as you travel northeast into the heartland of Pennsylvania, hooking up with Route 120, the Bucktail Highway, a winding rope of new asphalt, tall trees, crystal blue skies, edged with jagged mountain ridges.

I stopped for a drink at Whitcomb's Country Store, a red and white shingled structure with log facing and rows of elk antlers in the windows. Inside, along with the packaged goods, homemade sausage and pickles, the fishing tackles and postcards, a life-sized wooden Indian lounges in a swivel chair. On the wall, there's a photo of a deer under a quilt in a four-poster bed and another photo of an old man French-kissing a buck elk.

As I continued northeast, there were freshly painted houses, many of them red, valleys scooped out of burly hills, silver silos gleaming like rockets, coal tipples, raw wood barns hunching in fields of grain, glazed golden with sun. There were ferns wafting up over the shoulder of the road, huckleberry bushes, blankets of ivy. The pungent aroma of pine filtered through the heat.

Every time I ride through this part of the country, I am simultaneously invigorated and enchanted. The sights I see and the solace I experience remain with me long after I return home. This isn't gold or silver or the glory of Tom Mix, but it's treasure enough.

"Back road journeys do not end any more than a book ends because it has been read or a symphony because it has been heard or a painting because it has been seen," writes Ed Peterson. "In highway driving the trip is ended when the destination has been reached, but in backroad driving the trip lives on for many years, growing both in pleasure and in significance, for backroad driving is a belief in the abiding pleasure of blue sky and clouds, of a sparrow's song at night, of a stone house with a story to tell, of an old woman in a country store, a little girl who talked to a turtle, trillium in the spring and sumac in the fall, the taste of huckleberries, the smell of autumn apples, and the exhilaration of being lost and found again on an earth that, to those who live it, is always familiar."

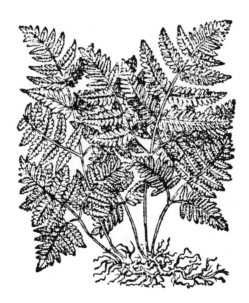

Knights of the Road

IT is nearly 3 A.M., the middle of an endless
night and day for the men gathered at the truck
stop just off Route 80, Clearfield County. There
are no pictures on the walls or music pumped from
sedate speakers in this murky, neon-framed diner—
just cement block, painted powder blue, and the
steady crackle of grease playing from the grill.

"God knows it might have been me," said Blackie.
"I wasn't more than two hundred yards behind him."

"Ed drove for ARCO, didn't he?" asked Wilson.

"I think," said Ryan.

Blackie sunk deep in a lumpy, plastic-covered
bench seat and shook his head. "I don't know
what happened, but suddenly the rig was a ball
of fire. I felt the heat first, then a sound . . .
WHOOOOOOSH . . . then I saw the flames; it was
sickening."

"Maybe it was a cigarette."

"He didn't smoke."

"Or a bullet."

"Who knows?"

There is a respectful silence as the men clean
fingernails with the corners of matchbooks, trap ciga-

110

rette ashes that have settled in their coffee spoons, or glance around the large room. Dozens of truckers can be found here at any time, eating eggs and bacon, or the T-bone steak special with toast, American fries, cole slaw, pie, and coffee for four dollars and tip. It isn't the quality of the food that lures truckers to this and similar stops along the highway, but the quantity and price—and the sign informing all travelers that "truckers will be seated and served first."

The men sitting at the counter or nearby booths listen to the conversation without comment, preoccupied perhaps by their own horror stories. The steelhauler remembers a friend mashed into a dashboard by five eight-ton girders jarred loose in an emergency stop. The LNG driver trembles at the thought of freezing to death in a wave of liquid nitrogen brought on by a crash. The teamster from Pittsburgh still dreams of the crater blown into the Pennsylvania Turnpike when a sniping trucker put a bullet into a scab dynamite truck. And only the very young haven't at least once witnessed an overturned load of animals, blood and flesh slicking the pavement, police gunning down crippled beasts.

"A trucker is in most danger in the mountains," explains Roy Watson, "and going down a mountain is more dangerous than going up. First, because your brakes might give out. Then you better hope no one's in your way and that somewhere near there's a 'runaway road.' That's a dirt escape ramp with a sandpile at the end. It'll stop forty tons. Then there's a chance of a jackknife—when your tractor is holding the road, but your trailer is out of control on ice, bending around and coming up parallel to the cab. The only thing to do then is to slam through the gears

111

and beat the floor. You've got to race it to win—because if the trailer gets ahead, you've had it."

"Every cargo has its own danger," said Don Craft. "Gravel's too heavy, grain is too light, animals too unstable. But I'll haul anything if the money's good, including dynamite. Even with explosives you can be blown out of danger. But with gasoline in an accident," he said, motioning over to Blackie, Wilson, and Ryan at the counter, "you're no better off than a roasting pig."

"I swear to God," Blackie was saying, sitting up and spreading his arms wide for emphasis. "I pulled over and ran as close as I could to the cab. The heat was murderous. A state trooper came up, and we could see Ed inside, but we couldn't do a damn thing about it." Blackie ground his cigarette with a silver-tipped cowboy boot into the cracked linoleum floor. "I heard Ed above all the noise. Sirens and horns were blaring and there were little explosions as small pockets of fuel hit flame. But I heard him. He was begging the trooper to shoot."

It is Sunday morning and more than a dozen men have gathered with their hats in their hands in the dusty parking lot to participate in a service that ends three minutes after it begins. John Huested, a transient of seventy-five, who visits more than ten such stops up and down the interstate on each day of rest, stands hatless and hairless behind an old battered Bible resting on a portable podium in the bed of his pickup truck. He is not a man to mince words or waste time with benign benedictions.

"Raise up your arms and your eyes, my brothers," he calls in his steady, even evangelistic voice. "You are men who live by chance and in jeopardy, men in isolation, like the nomads of Jerusalem. You deserve to die, you know, you dare death every day. Your only hope is to cast your lot with the Lord. Listen, you high-trippers," Huested calls, as if he is trying to hail men a half mile away. "Raise up your arms, let the Lord grasp your hand."

Two men in T-shirts and dungarees, their arms in the air, move forward, then drop to their knees almost in unison in front of the truck. The others remain standing but reach toward the sky.

"Do you believe?" asks the preacher softly.

"I believe," says one of the men on the ground.

"The road through life is perilous," says Huested, his thin black tie blowing in the wind. "Only with the Lord can you ride safely through it."

There is a long silence then, as the men bow their heads and pray in the dusty lot. The service ends when Huested nods, pockets his Bible, starts his vehicle, and pulls back on the highway, rear tires spitting gravel, as he makes for another chance congregation.

Buzztail Bagger

WHEN John E. (Baldy) Lee was bitten last year on his right forefinger at the finals of the Pennsylvania Rattlesnake Sacking Championship competition at Sinnemahoning Creek in north central Pennsylvania, he calmly retreated from the pit area, sat down on a nearby bench—and waited.

As the minutes ticked by, and the sun steamed in the haze above the hills, Blady's throat went dry, and his lips began to go numb. His eyes swelled shut. He had difficulty breathing. The world was suddenly a cave of searing flames and awesome shadows. As he stumbled toward the arriving ambulance, pain flashed through his body like a thousand bee stings. "First I lost control of my bowels, and then I started heaving. When we got to the hospital I was all empty, but still couldn't stop trying to turn myself inside out."

Baldy received seven vials of antivenom and was immediately airlifted to a larger medical facility, where he was injected with three additional doses. "My whole body was swollen. I was black and blue all over. My hand looked like one of them rubber gloves, blown up to bursting. The pain was so excruciating, I would have cried out loud. But," he paused to lower his voice, shrug his shoulders and bite his lip. "There were women around."

Of the twenty-three species of snakes in Pennsylvania, only three—the massasauga rattler, the timber rattler, and the copperhead—are poisonous. But in nearly four decades of snakehandling all over the country, Baldy had never before been bitten.

"When I was in the emergency room, the doctor told the nurse, 'Watch him, because he's going into shock.'

"'No way,' I said. 'That's full of shit!'

"I had always wondered what people went through when they got themselves bit, and I wasn't about to let myself go under now that I could find out.

"Years ago, a piece of steel flew into my eye and cut it in two. But I was never knocked out or anything," says Baldy, a foreman at Kaiser Aluminum in Erie when the accident happened. "I immediately made up my mind not to give into the pain." Since then, Baldy has worn a glass eye.

He is short, broad-shouldered, and bald, except for a rim of gray-brown hair encircling a shiny red crown. Whiskers hang like fringe from his chin, connecting his ears. As he talked, Baldy shuffled from foot to foot, self-consciously shrugging and blushing, in some ways resembling one of Snow White's dwarfs. But in no way is he funny looking. His arms and shoulders bulge with muscle. He is anchored low to the ground like an anvil.

For the snakehunts that precede the sacking competition, men armed with long-handled poles with metal hooks or pincers at the end—pinning forks—fan out into the hills, beating the bushes or poking under rocky shelves. Although their eyesight is poor, rattlers sense enemies through a device that works like a stethoscope, picking up vibrations from the ground. When it strikes it does so through heat sensors—facial pits located on both sides of the head. Sight doesn't determine the speed or accuracy of its bite, however; it is lightning fast. A car with the acceleration of a striking rattler would go from zero to sixty miles per hour in half a second.

In the northern United States, snakehunting and sacking are by far most popular in Pennsylvania, where prizes are awarded to hunters bringing in the largest snake, the snake with the most rattles (little beads in a sack at the tail, made of the same stuff as fingernails which, when vibrating, produce a buzzing sound similar to sizzling bacon). The biggest prizes go to hunters catching the most snakes and the smallest snake, usually hardest to handle. The rattler that bit Baldy was just thirty-nine inches long.

Baldy, who was in the hospital for a week and could squeeze pus out of his fingers for months afterward, now admits he had that bite coming. "I was much too rough with the snake. But hell, it was during the sacking, and I had a tough time to beat, if I expected to win."

For the competition, the sacker is presented with a canvas sack filled with five poisonous snakes, usually two copperheads and three rattlers. After dumping the snakes into the pit, he is allotted three minutes to calm them down, line them up—whatever. Meanwhile, a partner holds the sack. At the sound of the bell, the sacker plunges his hand into that hissing, squirming mass, picks up the snakes, and tosses them tail-first into the sack. The quickest time, often less than three seconds, wins.

Jacki Bibby of Rising Star, Texas, who lost most of his right thumb two years ago to a striking rattler, recently captured the national championship by bagging ten large diamondback buzztails in forty-five seconds. Diamondbacks are often as long as a man is tall and as thick as a weightlifter's arm. Sackers bitten once are penalized. Two bites and they are disqualified.

Although snakehunting and sacking have been branded as brutal and uncivilized by environmentalists and wildlife organizations, both activities are much tamer in Pennsylvania than most anywhere else. The Fish and Game Commission requires that reptiles be brought in alive and relatively unharmed, and subsequently released in good condition at the end of the weekend. The practice of squirting gasoline under rocks to flush the snakes out has been banned here for a long time. Recently, because a large number of snakes had been dying from fright and suffocation, the commission has prohibited the use of pinning forks to whip the snakes into sacks. Rules are considerably more relaxed elsewhere, however, especially in the South.

At the Claxton Tobacco Warehouse in Evans County, Georgia, bystanders can purchase the snakes caught by hunters, while at the rattlesnake roundup sponsored by the Waynoka, Oklahoma, Saddle Club, the refreshment stand does a large business in rattlesnake sandwiches. The nation's largest snaking event takes place each year at Sweetwater, Texas, the second weekend in March, when more than ten thousand diamondback rattlers are captured, milked of venom, butchered, and eaten. As an added incentive, snakers are paid a fee per pound as bounty.

Some rattlesnake roundups feature sideshows, where professional handlers putt coiled snakes like golf balls or hurl them thirty feet in the air, and catch them by the tail behind their backs. Bravery certificates are sometimes presented to spectators willing and able to milk a rattler. There are also beauty contests where women compete for the coveted crown of Miss Rattlesnake Rodeo at a Saturday night "Snakecharmer" dance.

Last year, his first at Sweetwater, Baldy not only single-handedly caught 108 diamondbacks, as many snakes as would have been collected in total during an average Pennsylvania hunt, but captured "the ugliest beard" award as well. "My wife and I were interviewed on television, appeared on the local news every night. People on the street—strangers— would come up and talk. That's what I like best about snakers. They're friendly, fantastic people."

An impartial observer might legitimately question Baldy's judgment. At Sinnemahoning this year, at least one hundred outlaw motorcyclists, skulls and crossbones tattooed on their shoulders, BORN TO BE FREE etched in silver rivets on leather vests, sat in siege around the perimeters of the compound, glowering and snarling, joking about beating up hippies, consuming many cases of beer. Additional dozens of outlaws were stewing their brains out in the bar directly across the road.

Five years ago, according to Cameron County's only narcotics officer, Glenn Fiebig, who is also the master of ceremonies for the snake sacking event, CBS News covered the sacking championship and, the following year, the area was blitzed by drunken, drug-crazed bikers. "We had a real riot on our hands." It has calmed down since then, however, primarily because Fiebig has loaded up the place with a couple of dozen deputy sheriffs, some working undercover as narcs. From the public-address system, atop the reviewing stand, Fiebig is constantly warning: "Any vulgar language or lewd displays will not be tolerated."

Despite the outlaws, Fiebig and most other snakers, including Baldy, maintain that snaking is a family affair. "Husbands and wives, fathers and sons, compete as teams," says Fiebig. Baldy's wife is a member of the board of directors of the Keystone Reptile Association. She makes the signs and banners for all events sponsored by the association, and decorates Baldy's clothes with silk-screened or needlepointed rattlers. Baldy's two daughters are also dedicated and experienced snake sackers.

"People say to me, 'Ain't it a little weird, you and the family spending all your free time playing with snakes?'

"'Well,' I tell 'em, 'maybe it is. But you take that guy in the funny red pants with nails in his shoes who beats the hell out of a little white ball all afternoon well, I think he's a little weird, too.'

"It's all in what your bag is, what you care about. With me, snakes are the most important creatures in my life."

Baldy claims that the snakehunts and sacking contests help preserve the species rather than destroy it. "A snake is like a loaded gun. It'll never do nothing to nobody, until somebody picks it up. Then there's bound to be trouble."

But isn't that exactly what sackers and hunters are doing? Simply provoking the snake?

"Maybe," Baldy admits, "But for good reason. You take people who watch a car race—just a bunch of cars running around in a circle. If the cars don't wreck now and again, nobody will go. It's the same thing here. The reason we have snake sacking is to bring people out. If we just laid out a bunch of snakes, no one would come and see them. Once they're here, we educate people about the importance and value of snakes. In Pennsylvania, snakes will soon be an endangered species because of how people mistreat them out of ignorance. So," Baldy concludes, "indirectly sacking can keep more snakes alive."

To be fair, there is a second pit area at Sinnemahoning where people can question experienced handlers as they play with the captured snakes, but the vast majority of spectators are glued tight around the refreshment stands, the T-shirt booths, and the sacking area.

Not all snakers agree with Baldy. In his paper, "Spare That Rattler," presented to members of Pittsburgh's Carnegie Museum Society, snakehunter Stephen Harwig says that the highlights of the weekend—exhibiting, measuring, handling—are show-off behavior which only demonstrates the accessibility of rattlers and the possibility of playing with them. Sacking actually decreases the rattlesnake population, according to Harwig. There are simply too many hunters and sackers for the snake population to absorb.

Although they are constantly arguing among themselves about the rules, the judgment of referees, the eyesight of timekeepers, and the publicity surrounding their sport, snakers are a tightknit group. They think snakesacking is dangerous, exciting, and challenging, and consider themselves courageous and special people—another variety of The Chosen

Few—for being an integral part of it. Members of the Keystone Reptile Association wear well-pressed khaki army shirts decorated with patches representing participation in snaking events all over the country. One small red patch is especially coveted, for it symbolizes membership in the Sunken Fang Society, exclusive to snakers who have been bitten and lived to talk about it.

Another patch, large and ostentatious, is displayed proudly by members of the Northcentral Pennsylvania Reptile Association, the host organization at Sinnemahoning. "This patch says it all," one snaker commented. "This is how we feel about each other and the rest of the world."

> IF YOU AIN'T A SNAKER,
>
> YOU AIN'T SHIT.

Teeth

AFTER breakfast, her husband looked up from across the table and announced that he was taking her into town to have all her teeth pulled out. It took a while for the meaning of his words to penetrate. Even when he said he was getting her a new set of teeth, she stared at him blankly. The memory of that morning nearly six months ago, pained her even now.

"My teeth ain't perfect, but they never give me or my husband no trouble," she said, rolling her eyes and shaking her head back and forth slowly. "And suddenly, there he wanted to go and pull them all out. I've never been so surprised in all my life."

She was sitting on a stoop in front of the tarpaper-covered cabin in which she and her husband lived, petting their old coon dog, curled in a grimy heap at her feet, and watching the tractor-trailer trucks whoosh by. Each time a truck went up the road, she would wave and smile. The truckers would invariably wave back, as they roared by, bellowing smoke.

She told me that her loneliness was sometimes awful. It wasn't the mountains—she had lived here all her life and wasn't interested in anywhere else—

but the fact that no one was around to talk to. The gloomy shadow that fell across her face blatantly telegraphed her desperation. Each time I visited, she went on and on, could hardly stop herself from talking.

She was a river of fat. Her body bulged and rippled in every direction, and her eyes, tucked into her pasty skin, looked like raisins pressed into cookie dough. Her hair was dirty gray, tangled and wooly, but you could tell her face had once been pretty. When she showed me her picture as an infant, I remarked that she looked like the Ivory Snow baby. Blushing, she covered her mouth and turned away. That was how we had first got on the subject of her teeth.

One day in town her husband was approached by the new dentist, a handsome young man in a white shirt and a blue and red striped tie, who explained that his house needed a new roof. Would he be interested in installing it in return for money or services?

Her husband was a short, wiry old man of seventy-two, who resembled a chicken hawk, with a hooked nose and arms that bowed out like furled wings. He hunched forward when he walked, as if he were about to take off flying. He told the dentist he would think on it for a while.

That evening, after supper, he stooped down and peered into her mouth, testing each of her teeth with his thumb and forefinger to see how well they were rooted. "Smile," he told her. "Laugh." She followed his instructions to the letter, as was her habit. Over the next few days, he watched her every chance he got. It was early autumn when he finally went back into town to make the deal. She never knew anything about it.

The woman explained that she and her husband had very little use for cash, bartering for almost everything they needed. They traded vegetables, cultivated on their tiny patch of land, for fruit—corn for peaches, tomatoes for apples, pickles for pears, beets for pretty bluefire plums. He chopped wood in return for mason jars. Periodically, he repaired a car for a guy who owned a dry goods store in town in exchange for clothes for the both of them. By bartering instead of buying and selling, they hardly paid Uncle Sam a penny's worth of taxes.

Last summer, he raised a barn for some city folks, recently retired near here, in return for an old engine from a '64 Buick and a side of beef. The engine went into a pickup truck they had gotten for one hundred fifty dozen eggs. Paid out over a period of three months, the eggs came from their chicken coops out back. The pickup was then swapped to the owner of a local filling station for credit for two hundred gallons of gas, plus an assortment of parts and tools. Meanwhile, she boiled up the beef on the old black cast-iron stove that had belonged to his grandfather, and canned and stored most of it in the cold-cellar cave under the house. She cut the remainder of the beef in strips and hung them like wet socks above the stove, smoking and shriveling them down to jerky. From the spring to the fall, her husband went fishing each evening after dinner. When he collected a big batch of trout, she stewed them in the pressure cooker until the whole fish, bones and all, was white and meaty like tuna. This was what they would eat next winter and the winters thereafter. Their cave was stocked with years of stuff.

Her husband never talked about his work and what was owed to him in the way of goods and services, and she never asked. Despite her significant contribution, the actual swapping wasn't her business. Years ago, her daddy had told her in no uncertain terms exactly what she needed to know to get herself through life. He was a man much like her husband, didn't owe anyone and never wasted anything. No words were said in conversation, unless there was some specific point to be made. Otherwise, silence was golden.

One night, however, her father came outside and squeezed down on the stoop beside her. They lived in an old house along the side of the road, about the same size as the one in which she and her husband lived now. But her father only rented it for fifty dollars a month. Neither her father nor his father before him had ever owned a piece of property straight out.

At the time, she didn't know that the old man was dying from cancer. Her mother had also died from cancer, and she had had to quit school in the sixth grade to take care of the rest of the kids and keep house. Recently, her two older brothers had joined the army, while the younger kids were sent to foster homes. Now, she and her father were home alone. She was fifteen at the time.

They sat side by side as the night grew colder. The moon shimmered in the glittering dish of sky, but the air felt like rain. Suddenly he cleared his throat. The sound of his voice made her feel uncomfortable, similar to how she felt trying on a new pair of boots.

"What else is there in life?" He said this as if in summation after a long conversation which she had somehow missed. Then, he paused. She would never forget his face as they sat there. His hard, sharp features seemed to disintegrate in the darkness. The

125

glitter reflecting from the moonlight faded from the blue of his eyes.

"You work to eat, you eat to live, you live to work." He sighed. "That's all there are to it."

The next morning, the man who was soon to become her husband made himself known. Miraculously, all of the details had been worked out between the man and her father in advance, without her having the slightest idea of what was happening. The following afternoon, the man came and took her away. Two weeks later, her father died.

She cleared her throat and motioned toward the house with her fat, flesh-soaked arm. "We came right here to these two acres and moved into an old shed out back. It ain't there no more. Tore it down to salvage the wood for this place. First we made sure we had good water, then we started building. From start to finish it took two years to get all set up. The winters were awful, but the summers weren't too bad."

All this happened some thirty years ago. Her husband had been married once before. His first wife died or left him, she wasn't sure, and his children, who she never met, were all grown up and living somewhere in another part of the state. Once in a great while, there was a letter, which he would read carefully, his lips moving, then stuff into his pocket, shaking his head and muttering. He would go on, muttering and cursing, shaking his head, for days at a time, without so much as an explanation.

Her own brothers and sisters all lived near here, but hardly ever stopped by or invited her to visit. Like most everyone else, they were more than a little afraid of her somber, silent husband.

Once again, she paused to wave at a trucker, barreling up the narrow two-lane highway. Their shack had been built unusually close to the asphalt. Even from up in the sleeping loft inside, you could hear the cinders and feel the wind when the trucks rumbled by. She said she was so shocked and angry when she found out about the deal her husband had made with the new dentist that she started screaming and yelling. "I had never acted that way before, but I just couldn't help myself. All of a sudden, I went crazy. My husband didn't know what to do."

He had turned away, glaring in silence out the window. It was still early. The sun was just beginning its ascent up the hill toward them. His eyes narrowed. Time passed as he stared down the road. His brows, thick and hairy, cast a shadow, like umbrellas over his eyelids. When the sunlight reached up as far as their house, he got up and finished dressing. He bit off a plug of tobacco, stuffed it under his cheek, put on his old grimy baseball cap, climbed into his pickup, and turned her over. When he saw his wife come out onto the porch, he threw the truck into reverse, backed up, and leaned out the window. He wanted to have his say one more time. "We shook hands on a new set of teeth. It's owed to me."

She turned and walked back into the house without a word. He peeled out onto the asphalt, his tires spitting gravel.

In no time, her best clothes were out of the drawer and piled on the bed. She found an old suitcase, cleaned it inside and out carefully, before laying in her clothes. The last time she had been on any sort of trip was when her husband had come to take her from her daddy. They didn't have a suitcase then. All her possessions, including her mother's big black roasting pan, fit easily into a medium-sized cardboard box. Her father carried the box down to the road and they waited together until the man who was to become her husband arrived. The whole thing— packing, waiting, and driving away—all took about ten minutes. It went by in a blur, one moment stacked up on top of another.

Thinking back, she realized that her life had ended right about then. She had been isolated with this man who hardly talked to her and whom she hardly knew, a man who had refused to discuss his past for over thirty years. At least with her father there was evidence of some roots and another life somewhere behind the one he had been living. But this man's world was bleak, both behind and beyond. He offered little more than a nod or a grunt for sustenance each day. Her father's words, uttered with such sadness and resignation on that damp, dark night so many centuries ago, came back to her now. *You work to eat, you eat to live, you live to work. That's all there are to it.*

All right. She had lived her life in accordance with her father's wishes, had never asked for anything from anyone, never shirked her responsibilities or wasted a breath. She had always done whatever her husband had told her to do—and more. But giving up a part of her own body simply for the sake of a business deal was too much. It was going too far. A person has a God-given right to own certain things, especially when they were born with it.

The last thing she did before leaving was to go out to the pump house and peer into the mirror. The image she saw glaring back at her was awful. She was too old, too fat, and too dirty. But, if anything, her face had held up best of all. There was still a spark, a hint of the beauty that might have been.

Her daddy, who never had more than a dollar in his pocket at any one time, had always bragged that the Good Lord had made him rich by blessing him with a daughter with a million-dollar smile. Even now, she could hear the distant echo of his praise. She wasn't going to let that damn bastard she married squash the memory by pulling out her teeth.

She looked up at me. The shroud that had fallen over her face as she told her story momentarily lifted. "Used to be my husband would leave me alone from early morning until supper. But now, things is different. He's liable to ride by anytime, just to check and see if I'm still here. Sometimes I hide out behind the chicken coops and wait for him. When the house looks empty, he'll stop to see where I am. He always pretends he's come back for tools or materials, but I know I got him worried. It serves him right."

She dug her fingers into her scalp, shook her head vehemently, scratching simultaneously before continuing. "I left the house that morning, hitchhiked into town, and bought a ticket for Davenport, Iowa. Davenport was the only city in the state I could think of. My daddy traveled all over the country when he was younger. He told me you could drive for half a day in any one direction in Iowa and not see anything else but a green carpet of corn, just bending and stretching in the distance."

She pushed her big blubbery legs out into the grass, right near where the old coon dog was lying. Once in a while, the dog would thrash around and thump its tail against the ground. A couple of times, it pushed itself up and crawled over on top of us. The woman had on brown doubleknit slacks worn through at the knees. Her blouse was white with alternating pink and blue pastel stripes, although the colors were

129

graying from repeated washings. This was the outfit she wore as she climbed aboard the bus and headed toward Davenport. Her clothes looked a lot better back then, she said.

It took nearly three hours to get to Pittsburgh, where they stopped and idled in the depot for about forty-five minutes. She did not get off the bus. They stopped twice on the highway in Ohio and once more in Indiana, but she remained in her seat, guarding her suitcase.

"I tell you, I've never done so much thinking in my entire life as I did on that bus, looking through the window, reading the neon signs and watching the headlights from the cars. Most of the people around me were sleeping, and none of them were too friendly. Not that I tried to do much talking. To tell the truth, I was scared half to death."

She wasn't actually thinking, she explained, as much as she was dreaming—with her eyes open. Her window was like an imaginary TV screen, and she could see the images of her past reflected before her. She saw her father carrying the cardboard box down to the side of the road. As the cancer took its toll, he had shriveled up like an old root. Then she saw the man who was to be her husband pull up. He put the cardboard box into the bed of the truck, opened up the passenger door, and helped her inside.

"I remember looking right into his face as he done this, the first time I had ever looked him full in the face. And then, as I sat in the darkness on that bus, I pictured how he had looked earlier that morning when he leaned across the table and told me he was going to take away my teeth. And you know what? He was the same. Those thirty years we had spent together had bloated me like a balloon and wrecked up my face but, except for a little more gray in his whiskers, that bastard ain't changed one bit."

She paused, shook her head, chuckled, then shook her head again and again. It wasn't easy to suddenly accept the reality of what had happened. The shiny sadness of her life reflected in her eyes.

I looked away, down behind the tarpaper shack toward the outhouse across the field. It had a three-hole bench. There were four or five old cars dumped into a gully behind the outhouse and an abandoned windowless schoolbus, teetering on the edge.

"I never made it to Davenport," she said, after a while. "But I got all the way to Chicago. You ever been to the bus station in Chicago? More people there than I ever seen, all in one place. Half of them don't speak English, and none of them was white. The moment I got off that bus, seeing all them coloreds and hearing all that foreign commotion, I was completely confused. I was hungry, but didn't want to spend any money. I also wanted to clean up a little, but with all them people, I was afraid to make a decision."

After a while, she found herself a bench back in the corner, out of the way, and sat down to try to think things out. She still had her ticket to Davenport, Iowa, but didn't particularly want to go there any more. She didn't want to go anywhere, as a matter of fact. She wasn't willing to move one inch from where she was. She must have dozed off, for the next thing she remembered was feeling a hand on her shoulder, shaking her gently. Someone was saying her name. No one would know her name in Chicago, so maybe she really was back home, about to emerge from a terrible dream.

But when she finally opened her eyes, an elderly

131

man with horn-rimmed glasses and a tiny, pinched nose introduced himself as a representative of the Traveler's Aid Society, whatever that was. The man's voice was soft and reassuring. As he talked, he picked up her bag, wrapped his arm around her ample shoulders, helped her up, and led her across the bus station.

When her husband had discovered her missing, the man explained, he had contacted their minister, who somehow traced her to Pittsburgh, and subsequently to Chicago. There was also a Traveler's Aid representative waiting at the Davenport bus station, just in case she had made it that far.

They were moving at a brisk pace, passing the ticket counters and neatly wending their way through the milling crowd. She felt like a piece of livestock. "Where are you taking me?"

"There's a bus to Pittsburgh leaving in about ten minutes. Your husband already wired the money." He smiled and continued to talk to her in his quiet and reassuring manner, as they pushed through a big set of swinging doors and headed on down a broad cement runway toward a long line of idling buses. Drivers in neatly pressed gray uniforms stood by the doors of their respective vehicles puffing cigarettes and punching tickets, as she and the man hurried by.

"But I already have a ticket to Davenport, Iowa."

"You can cash it in when you get back home . . ." He paused, all the while continuing to lead her down along the row of buses. "Of course, I can't force you to do anything you don't want to do." He shrugged and smiled apologetically. "I can't even help you make up your mind."

By this time, they were approaching the bus to

Pittsburgh. She felt his hand on her back, urging her gently toward the bus. He handed a ticket and her suitcase to the driver.

Meanwhile, she hesitated, momentarily resisting the pressure on her back. She tried desperately to think things out, but her mind was blank, as was her future.

With nothing better to do, she walked up the steps, dropped into a seat by the window, and closed her eyes. She did not allow herself to open her eyes until hours later, when the bus pulled into Pittsburgh. She was so confused and embarrassed, she had completely forgotten to say good-bye to the man with the horn-rimmed glasses who had helped her.

Now she looked up at me, smiling and winking. "My husband came to meet me." The thought evidently amused her, for she shook her head back and forth, chuckling. "On the way home, we talked things over, got everything out in the open for the very first time. I told him how lonely I was, how it wasn't fair the way he constantly mistreated me. I said that I should be consulted in his decisions about how we spend our money. I told him that I didn't have enough clothes, that I wanted to go into town more often, and that, because he was such a damn hermit, I didn't have no friends or family." She nodded emphatically. "I let him have it with both barrels. He had never allowed no one to talk to him that way before in his entire life."

I stood up. More than two hours had passed since we had first started talking. The sky was clouding over. In this part of western Pennsylvania, rain erupts suddenly, swallowing the hillsides and ravaging the roads. Besides, I was getting cold, sitting so long on that stoop. And my pants were filthy, where

133

the old coon dog had tracked mud all over me. I walked briskly back to my motorcycle.

"He tries to be nice," she said, as she followed along behind me. "But you really can't change him. You couldn't ever change my daddy either," she added. "When you come right down to it, they was both dark and silent men."

I nodded, pulled on my helmet and kicked down on the starter. The machine cranked to life as I straddled the seat. From past experience, I knew that I couldn't wait for the right moment to leave. Otherwise I'd be waiting forever. I had to depart even while she was still in the act of talking.

She planted her foot in my path and grabbed my arm. "You know, he drove by two or three times while we was sitting here talking. He'll want to know who you are and everything was said. Hell," she said, smiling and winking, finally stepping out of the way, so that I could pull out, "I ain't telling him nothing. It serves him right."

The woman prepared herself extra special for her husband's homecoming that evening.

She went into the pump house and sponged herself down from head to toe, ran a brush through her hair a hundred times, scrubbed the grime from her fingers until the half-moons of her nails were white. Back in the house, up in the loft where they slept, she got out the nice green cotton jumper dress with the pretty yellow and white floral design and laid it out on the quilt. He had bought her the dress the day she came home. She had only taken it out of the box once, the following Sunday when they went to church.

After preparing dinner and setting the table nice and neat, she went back upstairs and put on the

134

dress. Then she dusted herself with some fancy-smelling powder she had ordered through a magazine and gotten in the mail. She was just about ready, when his truck crackled outside on the gravel. He walked into the house. She could hear him move about downstairs, looking into the big pot on the cast-iron stove, sniffing what was for dinner. But not until he walked across the room and started up the ladder toward the loft, did she reach into the water glass on the nightstand beside their bed. Only then did she put in her new teeth.

Author's Note

I met most of the people in this book accidentally, sipping beer from bottles in dim taverns, working the woods, walking along dusty country roads. It took time and patience to wait for their stories, but in the process I made friends and learned things I wouldn't have necessarily known, not only about deer, rattlesnakes, and firewood, but also about loneliness and human nature.

This is how I experienced Penn's Woods West— how you should experience it—spontaneously, unhurriedly, without preconceived notions, schedules, outlines, plans. Come into the country when you feel the urge. Wander for a weekend. Return for an afternoon. Remain for a week. I listened to the sounds and the voices, breathed the air, absorbed the rough and smooth edges of the place in small and pleasurable doses.

After a decade of wandering, I began to write about the people who shared their lives and dreams with me. Although I occasionally changed names and altered locations, hardly anyone requested anonymity; I simply felt they deserved it.

I don't think these stories are unique to western

136

Pennsylvania. I have touched almost every corner and crevice of the country on my motorcycle and have come to believe that independence and eccentricity are national traits. Wherever you go, listening is the cornerstone of communication.

What distinguishes western Pennsylvania from everywhere else, however, is the kaleidescope of people who have emerged here over the years, so close to a major metropolitan area. From Pittsburgh, an hour on good roads in any of a dozen directions will put you simultaneously in sight of the past and in touch with the future. It is this inviting integration of tradition and accomplishment, tragedy and innocence, beauty and devastation, that makes Penn's Woods West and its people so special.

Pittsburgh, Pennsylvania
March 27, 1983

Other books by Lee Gutkind:

Bike Fever
The Best Seat in Baseball, But You Have to Stand!
God's Helicopter (a novel)

and the film
A Place Just Right